Heart Wisdom

Daughters of the King
Bible Study Series

Cover and Interior Design: Derinda Babcock
Editor(s): Susan K. Stewart, Deb Haggerty
Author Represented By: Shawn Kuhn, SuzyQ Media

Published by Elk Lake Publishing, Inc., Plymouth, Massachusetts 02360, 2019

Library Cataloging Data
Names: [Miller, Kathy Collard] (Kathy Collard Miller)
Heart Wisdom—A Daughters of the King Bible Study/ Kathy Collard Miller
166 p. 23cm × 15cm (9in × 6 in.)

Description: Wisdom for living is one of God's wonderful provisions and there's no greater collection of wisdom than in the biblical book of Proverbs.

Identifiers: ISBN-13: 978-1-950051-65-6 (trade paperback) | 978-1-950051-66-3 (POD) | 978-1-950051-67-0 (e-book)
Key Words: Proverbs, Wisdom, Knowledge, Inspirational, Devotional, Trusting God, Women
LCCN: 2019940498 Nonfiction

Endorsements

People are talking about Kathy Collard Miller's *Daughters of the King Bible Study Series* and *Choices of the Heart...*

Kathy Collard Miller's *Choices of the Heart* is a Bible study full of sound scriptural principles, balanced spiritual wisdom, and a deep understanding of what matters most to women. Miller's study makes great use of an all-star, all female cast of leaders falling on both sides of the spiritual and moral equation. Her insightful questions invite the reader to reflect on her own life within a scriptural framework—prompting growth from the heart. I can't wait to use *Choices of the Heart* with my own women's Bible study.

I'm looking forward to more from Kathy Collard Miller!
—Catherine Finger, Ed.D,
Speaker and author, the *Murder with a Message* series

With each lesson, I was invited to recognize that choices of the heart aren't simple or defined without the grace of God. Each account of women in the Bible in this Bible study lifts a layer of possible misconception, asserts refreshing challenges, and presents applications of God's Word, bold yet gentle. At times, the reader is tugged to examine the heart and analyze motives. But with each lesson, the exhortation is profoundly clear, leaving a pleasant reassurance that we women today do have much in common with women of the Bible. Yet, we are called to learn from their examples to make godly choices as daughters of the King who dance to the melody of his redeeming love.
—Janet Perez Eckles,

Author, *Simply Salsa: Dancing Without Fear at God's Fiesta*

Choices of the Heart from bestselling author Kathy Collard Miller is a must-read for all women who desire to walk in God's light as they become more like Jesus. This is not only a well-written book, but it is also laid out in such a way that it can be used by both individuals and groups. Highly recommended!

—Kathi Macias,
Multi-award-winning author of more than 50 books, including *The Singing Quilt* and *Return to Christmas*

Kathy Collard Miller thoughtfully addresses choices and attitudes that undermine or set us free. With encouragement and warmth, she helps us choose God's way and blessing. This exploration of biblical lives and choices can change your life.

—Judith Couchman,
Author, *Designing a Woman's Life* book, Bible study, and seminar

As the founder of Modern Day Princess Ministries I am always looking to recommend resources for women that further the depth of our walk with Christ. The Daughter of the King series by Kathy Collard Miller does exactly that. It enables you to discover the wealth you have in knowing the King of Kings as your Heavenly Father and begin walking in the royalty you possess.

—Doreen Hanna,
Treasured Celebrations, founder & president

Choices of the Heart provides excellent insight and instruction for the Christian woman who longs for more of God's Word. The women of the Bible come alive as they tackle life issues and struggles that are relevant to today's world. Kathy Collard Miller is a name you can trust for great Bible teaching.

—Laura Petherbridge, Speaker, author, *The Smart Stepmom, 101 Tips for The Smart Stepmom*, and *When I Do Becomes I Don't—Practical Steps for Healing During Separation and Divorce*

Kathy Collard Miller's new study, *Choices of the Heart*, gives us a treasure chest of encouragement and wisdom for a glorious life. Whether we struggle with the grittiness of jealousy, temptation or unforgiveness, Kathy points us to God who always gives us the power to move us into a meaningful pathway. I love the way Kathy takes the participant through the journey of examining the lives of women in the Bible and revealing the outcome of their bad and wise choices.

This is a great study for personal reflection during a devotion time or for discussions in a larger group setting. Kathy has done stellar research and written a masterpiece crafted to enrich the reader's knowledge of the Bible and their spiritual life.

—Heidi McLaughlin,
International speaker and author of *Sand to Pearls*, *Beauty Unleashed* and *Restless for More*

At the crux of every circumstance, we have two basic choices: whether to trust and whether to obey—intentional decisions to yield to God and embrace his Word. Kathy captures this powerful truth in *Choices of the Heart*. She invites us to walk with God in the great adventure of life, encouraged along the journey by our Heavenly Father's love and faithfulness. Such a motivating study!

—Dawn Wilson, Founder, Heart Choices Today,
San Diego, California, president, Network of Evangelical Women in Ministry (NEWIM)

Dedication

To Wes and Nancy Anderson—whose spiritual impact, example, and wisdom have been precious to me. I praise God for you.

Acknowledgments

Back in the 1990s, Mary Nelson of Accent Publications saw the potential of my idea for a women's Bible study series. With her guidance, the twelve-book study in the *Daughters of the King Bible Study Series* was created. I was grateful for her leadership.

Now, I'm thrilled Deb Haggerty has understood and supported my vision of expanding the initial simple format to include commentary and greater depth for every book in the series. Thank you, Deb. Your leadership of Elk Lake Publishing Inc is phenomenal, and you are the Publisher of the Year in my book! You bless me with confidence and encouragement.

Susan K. Stewart of Practical Inspirations has been a delight to work with as she edited and wisely guided me toward communicating clearly the truths of Scripture. Susan, you have a gentle yet skillful ability, and I so appreciate your responsiveness.

I value having my agent, Shawn Kuhn, on my team of support and wisdom. Thank you, Shawn, for being available.

I'm so grateful for the love and encouragement from my husband, Larry. Honey, let's make it another forty-nine years walking this journey together! You make God look good.

Heart Wisdom

A Ten Lesson Study in the
Daughters of the King
Bible Study Series

Kathy Collard Miller

PUBLISHING THE POSITIVE
ELK LAKE PUBLISHING INC
Plymouth, Massachusetts

Contents

Introduction

Heart Wisdom is a study of the book of Proverbs. Even though topics are not grouped together within Proverbs, there are themes running through that book of wise sayings penned by God's control through several supernaturally led men of God, primarily Solomon. Each of the ten lessons in this Bible study focus on one or more topics covered within those sayings.

I've used the English Standard Version (ESV) as the basis for answering questions.

—Kathy Collard Miller

Edit needed at bottom of p.13

Lesson 1

Proverbs about Words

Words are powerful. The old saying, "Sticks and stones may break my bones, but words will never hurt me" is false. God knew from the beginning the power of words. God's very words created our world and all the galaxies. And Jesus himself, the second person of the Trinity, is called the Word. Yes, words are powerful.

God created words for his created human beings to be used in meaningful and powerful ways for good. In contrast to God's words of blessings and creativity are Satan's words of temptation for evil. Even in the Garden of Eden, words were misused and misunderstood. Eve listened and believed Satan's words, and pain and destruction were created. What a sad beginning.

But God was not surprised nor overwhelmed. From eternity, he knew the plan to send Jesus as Savior for the sin of mankind. Jesus declared, "It is finished," and communicated with words redemption had been accomplished.

Words are important vehicles for God's use. No wonder God caused Solomon to include so much wisdom about words in Proverbs. We can grow in our ability to use words to bless others and glorify God.

Let's begin our study of Proverbs about this important subject by thinking about the impact of words in our own lives.

1. What is the <u>most</u> encouraging thing someone has said to you? *4/19*

Katelyn's email "Thank you so so so so so so much for the coolest gift that has ever been given in the history of gifts. I love you so much!!!"

A. What has been the most discouraging thing someone has said to you?   " "We have a cow chewing cud in our class",

Mr. Hodges - ASU - You sit there in class with a poker face.
" I'll kill you". " You'll have to find another hairdresser."

receive backlash from it.

B. Why do we sometimes find it hard to keep our words loving and kind? We speak before we think

C. What <u>different desires</u> can motivate us to offer the appropriate words for the setting? • A desire to <u>not offend someone</u>,
• A desire to be in God's will + not grieve his Holy Spirit.
• A desire to speak life into another's life.
• A desire to know the joy that comes when speaking words that build up another.

2. What is God's perspective of words as indicated in <u>Proverbs 18:21?</u>
" Death and life are in the <u>power of the tongue</u>, They that love (it) shall eat the fruit thereof. "

Purposes back of book - 15r page

A. How do you think people can <u>misuse the ideas</u> of Proverbs 18:21?
* Using the tongue to speak death into a life is a misuse of God's intention. However another thought is speaking death to the <u>self nature</u> can bring life to the New Nature

B. How best does God want Proverbs 18:21 to be used?

To speak <u>Life</u>

Guard it. Don't let it become bitter.

3. How does Proverbs 4:23 offer a balancing perspective for a person who receives damaging words?
" <u>Keep</u> thy heart with all diligence; out of it are the issues of life. "

Is. 54:17 Every tongue that 4 shall rise against you in judgement — thou shalt condemn.

Jesus indicated the importance of words when he said, "I tell you, on the day of judgment people will give account for every careless word they speak" (Matthew 12:36). If Jesus speaks of such judgment, we can be sure our words make a huge impact. We should carefully evaluate not only our words, but also our body language, tone, and actions. Most importantly, we must be aware of our motives. Do we truly desire to see God glorified in our interactions?

Yet sometimes Proverbs 18:21 is misused and misunderstood as if words force someone to act a certain way or be affected in a certain way. After all, if words are so powerful, maybe someone has power over me, or I can force her to respond the way I want. People can say or think, "When she said that, I was compelled to respond in that negative way, so it's not my fault." Or "He doesn't say loving words, so I have every right to feel unloved." But every person has a choice as to how to respond to damaging and/or encouraging words.

For instance, if someone tells us we are speaking in an unchristian manner, the assessment could be true or false. Perhaps, they don't like the righteousness we stand for. We could even be suggesting they turn away from sin, something for their good, but they are resistant.

To evaluate whether our words are godly, we should ask ourselves, "What is really true? Does God want me to respond this way or not?" We can have the confidence to know God knows the right words and judges rightly. Strangely enough, even words of praise could be damaging to someone if she depends upon praise for her worth and value, rather than seeing herself as God sees her "in Christ."

Proverbs 4:23 gives us the balancing perspective. We need to guard our hearts from impure motives. And yet every person who hears encouraging or discouraging words is responsible to guard their own hearts. Only God can determine if any words are true, applicable, and whether they should be believed and acted upon.

4. What does God say should not characterize our conversations in Proverbs 4:24?

A crooked mouth or perverse lips

A. What does that mean to you?

I should not say anything about someone behind their back that I wouldn't say to their face. I should say nothing that insinuates anything negative or belittling another.

B. Why is that important?

Because when I do it, flesh is ruling and the Spirit is grieved. Others may be hurt - relationships are strained.

In Hebrew, the word "crooked" (ESV) means distortion, twisting of the truth, perverse things, and anything contrary to the law of God or the Gospel of Christ. It's easy to deceive ourselves thinking our words are pure when actually, we are hurting others and not obeying God's guidance for responding to another person.

For instance, we can easily think we aren't hurting anyone when we're exaggerating. Or we can distort the truth by omitting some facts and including those which favor us. We might misrepresent others' words. We can omit someone's side of the conversation. We could repeat someone's words with a different tone of voice distorting their intentions. These possibilities grow when we think of technology. Emails, texts, and social media posts can all fuel miscommunication.

5. What wrong responses are pointed out in Proverbs 26:22–26, 28?

Proverbs 26

A. vs. 22: *Tale bearing - whispering - gossiping - that goes down into the deeper parts.*

B. vs. 23: *Lips that are burning with anger or eagerness to tell - they may be clothed with a sweet tone*

C. vs. 24: Dissembleth   H 5234

This causes deceit within

D. vs. 25:   Sweet words - pleasant words
   but with a heart full of
ungodly motives - (7 abominations in the
heart)
hatred, jealousy, envy, hypocrisy, ...

E. vs. 26:
      hatred covered by deceit -
(words like honey - war in heart)

F. vs. 28: lying , flattering

G. If any, which ungodly response do you sometimes struggle with?
   I say things to others that I would not
say to the person face to face.

H. How would you like to accept God's help in that area?
   By convicting me before I do it and giving
me strength and wisdom to refrain.
(Sunday was a ½ way example with Thurman -
about the painting that he thought was not paid for.

6. Proverbs 6:12–19 describe a person who is displeasing to the Lord. What word does 6:12 use to describe this person overall?

   One who sows discord

A. What are other characteristics:

B. vs. 12: perverse mouth

C. vs. 13-14: uses his eyes, feet +
fingers - to show perversity in his
♡ eyes - winking
(fingers demonstrating a person talking too much or nagging
- feet - kicking a person under the table to
D. vs. 18: stop them from speaking.

a ♡ that devises wicked imaginations -
ex. nancy with karen -

E. vs. 19: false **witness** that speaks lies
and sows discord.

F. What will happen to this person (vs. 15)?

He shall be broken without remedy

G. What seven things does God add (16-19)?
a proud look (feeling of superiority), lying,
violence, ♡ that devises wicked imaginations,
killing feet swift to do mischief, a false witness that
speaks lies + sowing discord.

H. If any, which ungodly description do you struggle with? How
would you like to correct it?
sowing discord by speaking words that
don't build up - pointing out Ed's harshness
instead of pointing out his strengths.

I. Which one do you struggle with the least?

hands that shed innocent blood

7. Counteract the ungodly *with godly* descriptions of Proverbs 6:12–19 in the following situations by giving ideas for positive talking:

That come from positive thinking

A. with your husband or boyfriend.

Instead of words that sow discord – words that bring unity –

B. with each of your children (name each one specifically).

Jon –
Jeff –

C. with your parents. *—————*

D. with your siblings.

Pam   – Build up & help with Jim

E. with a particular friend.

Judi

9

F. with a particular coworker or boss.

The visual depiction (vs. 13) of a person winking, signaling with his feet, or pointing with his finger can be confusing. The Hebrew words refer to a person who adds to what he is saying with the motive of making false, confusing, or deceptive suggestions. His simple words really can't be trusted.

The Proverbs writer is warning the winking man should be regarded as sneaky and untrustworthy. Often such a person says one thing but later claims he was misunderstood if he is held to what he said. He refers to his body language confirming the different meaning.

Just imagine a woman criticizing someone but not mentioning her name, yet she points with her hand or even foot to who she is talking about. Later, she can say she didn't say the name and did nothing wrong.

8. What contrasts do you see between righteousness and foolishness regarding the tongue and words?

PROVERBS 10

Verse in Proverbs 10	The Righteous or Wise	The Foolish or Wicked
vs. 11	mouth is a well of life	mouth covered by violence
vs. 12	Love covers sin	Hate stirs up strife
vs. 13	wisdom comes to one w/ understanding	The rod comes for one void of understanding
vs. 14	wise men lay up knowledge	mouth of a fool is close to destruction
vs. 15	A rich man's wealth is his strong city	Destruction of poor is poverty
vs. 16	His work tends to life	The wicked's fruit is sin

[handwritten margin note: left- with the comment about "stupid"]

Verse in Proverbs 10	The Righteous or Wise	The Foolish or Wicked
vs. 17	keeping instruction is The way of life	despise correction & in doing so err.
vs. 18	does not hide hatred & lie	utters slander making him a fool.
vs. 19	refrains his words	speaks a multitude of words
vs. 20	His tongue is like choice silver	his heart is of little worth
vs. 21	His lips feed many	die for lack of wisdom

" Wonderful words of life "

9. From Proverbs 10:11, how would you describe "a fountain of life" coming from someone's words? refreshing

His words are pleasant to hear — cause the heart to delight and be strengthened to appreciate life - to be grateful - to love - To care - To want to be & do what brings life to another.

No doubt each one of us would describe such a fountain in different ways because words affect each person uniquely. What someone values might not be what another person values. What someone considers wise or encouraging words might not be what someone else thinks is positive. We each "hear" and "perceive" in different ways depending upon our past experiences, our beliefs, and/or our perceptions of truth.

Good communication and offering God's words of life require wisdom and sensitivity. Each one of us must seek God's direction and also feel free to ask others about meeting their needs. Here are some possible useful phrases:

- I'd love to hear what's going on. Would you like to share?
- How can I help you in a practical way? Would bringing over a meal be helpful?
- I know each of us grieves in different ways. How has this journey of loss been for you?
- When something like that happened to me, I felt like … But you are most likely feeling differently. How are you feeling?

Assuming you know what she should feel based on how you reacted is not offering a fountain of life. Or immediately talking about your own experience after she shares will communicate you aren't interested in hearing from her, only focusing on yourself. You may think you're adding to the conversation, but most people feel like their experience is being compared to yours.

Most often, the most helpful thing you can do is to talk little, even if there is silence. Romans 12:15 encourages us, "Rejoice with those who rejoice, weep with those who weep." James 1:19 urges us, "Know this, my beloved brothers: let every person be quick to hear, slow to speak, slow to anger."

Such godly responses are difficult because silence can make us feel uncomfortable. Saying nothing can seem like we aren't loving, serving, or caring about them. But most often erring on the side of less words than more is the best thing we can do.

10. What wisdom does Proverbs 10:8, 10, 19 give?

- A wise ♡ receives commandments
- A prating fool shall fall - a winking eye brings sorrow. He that refrains his lips is wise.

A. In what specific ways do you think "many words" make it easier to sin (10:19)?

many words can weary the listener.
many words indicate a self centered disposition that wants to speak rather than hear.
a barage of "?"s from another can also do damage.

B. What might too much talking indicate within the heart of the person talking?

self centeredness

C. What possible response can it bring within others?

weariness
impatience
a closed door for relating

12

D. For someone who seems to talk appropriately, what do you think enables her to have self-control and wisdom?

Open to the Holy Spirits leading, guidance + counsel. A true wanting to hear what another thinks or feels.

Too much talking can get someone in trouble. If someone talks excessively there could be many motivations. Maybe she feels like no one listens to her therefore she wants to get in her "two cents worth" at every possible opportunity. Or silence feels awkward, and she assumes everyone else feels awkward also. Therefore, it's up to her to rescue these uncomfortable people. But other people may actually be grateful for the silence.

Unfortunately, any of us can believe we talk just the right amount and we use the right words. Even the person who says little might be withholding because of insecurity or fear. None of us have a right to criticize the choices of others, but if someone monopolizes the conversation in a group, we can seek the Lord's direction, wisdom, and grace to share with her. We could also ask questions about what communication was like in her family growing up. Sometimes a child who was ignored or neglected can feel voiceless. Once grown up, she feels important and included when someone is listening to her. We can't judge, but we can reach out in love even as we seek God's perspective on what's appropriate in each situation and circumstance.

✱ Note: This last section has some omissions and 5 chapters that don't seem to fit here.

Women of the Bible

11. Priscilla was a friend of the Apostle Paul and a dedicated worker in the early church. Her words give us a picture of godly attitudes and actions representing Jesus. Describe how from these verses:

Edit needed.
Acts 18:24-28

A. Acts 18:1–3, ~~Proverbs~~ 24–28: *(Acts ?)*   *Acts 18:24-28*

She along with her husband took him in + they worked together making tents. Expounded the word of God more clearly to Apollos - an eloquent man - mighty in the Scriptures.

who knew only the baptism of John

13

B. Romans 16:3–4:

In helping – laid down their own lives. They helped in Christ Jesus.

C. I Corinthians 16:19:

They had church in their home.

12. What would you like to apply to your life this week from Priscilla's example?

Hospitality –
working together
Laying down my life to help another
Having church in the home.
Acts 18:36 • Expounding the way of God more perfectly.

A. In what ways did Priscilla's words reflect well on her relationship with Jesus?

Where is there o passage about her words? When Priscilla + Aquilla heard they
Acts 18:26 • Took him + expounded unto him the way of God more perfectly.

B. In what ways did she trust God enough to speak wisely with her words?

Implied – They took him unto them – They cared enough to "correct him" into a more accurate description of the way of God
By not overtly correcting him in public. By not judging him – by not leaving him with his limited understanding.

If Priscilla and Aquila hadn't trusted God, they might have responded critically directly to Apollos or talked behind his back to steer people away from him. Priscilla could have thought, "Aquila and I have to step in and correct this man because we must protect Jesus's reputation. I must make sure everyone knows the totally correct truth." Yet because she truly believed God was in control, God could take care of his own reputation. And because no one needed to be perfect to speak of Jesus, she didn't overreact and wound the passion of a new believer.

As a result, Priscilla and Aquila wisely took Apollos aside and gently gave him more complete information. They trusted God was big enough to protect his reputation from the errors of his representatives. And as a result, Apollos went on to be a significant evangelist (I Corinthians 3:5).

Apollos was receptive to Priscilla and Aquila's wisdom, but not everyone we encounter will be. All we can do is seek God's guidance in the words we say and then leave the results to him. That's trusting God with our words.

My precious Princess and Daughter:

Your words are very important to me. Just as you desire to hear an encouraging word, I want you to give encouraging words.

I understand how difficult that is at times. In so many circumstances and situations, I know you are tempted to use discouraging, harmful, or controlling words. But I know, too, your heart and your desire to reflect me.

Beloved daughter, you are my spokeswoman and so many need to hear words of truth. Never be afraid to speak like my princess. Isn't that more important and valuable than getting empty satisfaction from a few powerless, self-centered words? I will bless your words when they are centered in me.

Read my words. Absorb the fact of my great love for you, my plans for your good, and my perspective of your life. Know how important and valuable you are to me, my precious one. Don't ever forget even when hurtful things are said to you or about you, they are insignificant compared to who I say you are to me.

Lovingly,

Your heavenly Father, the King

Lesson 2

Proverbs about Anger and Conflict

As God inspired Solomon and other writers to pen Proverbs, we can be thankful God didn't avoid or diminish the difficult subject of anger and conflict. He knows humans will struggle with many areas of life and especially when trying to respond in a godly way toward anger and conflict.

From the very beginning in the Garden of Eden there were divisive responses. After Adam and Eve sinned, destruction began with the murder of one son by the other. Though so close to the point of creation, the son refused to call upon God for help with conflict and deal with his anger.

God didn't give up on his creation and gives practical help in Proverbs for anger. We have a choice about dealing with our human unpleasant emotions. We can choose destruction or act wisely as we trust God. Let's see what we can learn from the wonderful, practical Proverbs.

1. Do you believe anger is sin? **No**

   A. When would it be sin and when would it be acceptable?

a sin when it controls you and causes contempt in your heart toward MAN.
acceptable when angry over wrong r evil -
acceptable when it motivates to overcome evil w good.

   B. What do you see as the source of most anger and conflict...?

my thoughts - Pride - Evil

C. between people in general?

Self centeredness that doesn't get its way.

D. between men?

E. between women?

F. between men and women?

G. If there's a difference between these comparisons, why did you think so? *I don't see the differences*

The topic of whether anger is sin is controversial, complex, and creates misunderstanding. What makes it even more difficult is how people define anger. Sometimes we say, "I'm not angry, I'm just irritated." Or we play down the intensity or deny it completely. We justify anger thinking it's the only feeling available in a certain situation. We also may have trouble identifying emotions, especially anger. As a result, this potentially damaging feeling gets jumbled up with many other responses. It's hard to sort out.

For instance, gender differences can contribute. Women tend to get their point across by using emphasis in their words whereas men raise their voices. A woman might think a man is angry, but he would say he's just trying to communicate the importance of what he's saying. These are generalities but are overall true.

women raise their voices men emphasize words.

18

what culture does this?

Kathy Collard Miller

Different cultures think of anger and conflict differently. Certain nationalities take pride in their "passion" and consider yelling normal. Conflict might be handled by putting down the other person to intimidate and be powerful. But since all these practices are frequent and other patterns aren't modeled, children learn from the beginning to respond these ways without question.

Obviously, there are many underlying causes for anger and conflict. We might really wonder why God gave us the ability to be angry at all. He might have saved us lots of temptation if he hadn't. The truth is God gets angry, and we are made in his image. His anger and wrath are motivated by his hatred for sin and its destructive forces. His anger is pure and not sinful, because he only wants what is best for his creation, and he always takes action appropriately.

Unfortunately, our anger and fighting are based in wanting our own way. Our loving heavenly Father wants to teach us how to take the energy anger causes and use it to correct injustice and resist using anger for self-protective or ungodly means. Many verses in the Bible give God's perspective and practical direction.

For instance, Ephesians 4:26–27, 31–32 tell us, "Be angry and do not sin; do not let the sun go down on your anger and give no opportunity to the devil. Let all bitterness and wrath and anger and clamor and slander be put away from you, along with all malice. Be kind to one another, tenderhearted, forgiving one another, as God in Christ forgave you."

We can learn to respond in loving ways even though we are tempted to turn our anger into hurtful conflict. Paul's command of "Be angry and do not sin" (Ephesians 4:26) gives us a firm foundation: the emotion of anger is not necessarily sin in itself. It's how we respond to the initial feeling. We must deal with it by finding the cause and then in God's power seek God's answer.

2. In which of these areas do you experience the greatest temptation for anger and conflict? Rate each one 1 to 5 (5 meaning greatest).

A. husband or boyfriend

5

B. children

4

C. friends

2

D. siblings

1

E. boss or co-worker

1

F. church relationships

1

G. ministry relationships

1

H. parents

N.A.

If you have been told you are an angry person, yet don't see yourself in the same way, you may have to evaluate whether you creatively hide your anger from yourself through denial, dismissal, or justification. You may have to risk hearing your relative or friend's perspective. Anger is often difficult to identify in ourselves. Even conflict can be hard to identify. It just seems normal. Seeing the truth can take great trust in God's gentle Holy Spirit.

The Apostle Paul prayed, "I do not cease to give thanks for you, remembering you in my prayers, that the God of our Lord Jesus Christ, the Father of glory, may give you the Spirit of wisdom and of revelation in the knowledge of him, having the eyes of your hearts enlightened, that you may know what is the hope to which he has called you, what are the riches of his glorious inheritance in the saints" (Ephesians 1:16–18). God does want to answer that prayer for us to understand the truth of our motives.

Sacred Journey

3. Anger and conflict can be caused by many things. What possible sources do you find in the following Proverbs? What would the antidote be for each? The verse(s) may or may not supply the antidote, but think through what a godly response or behavior would be. *Love is the antidote for anger*

Verse(s)	Source of Anger	Antidote
3:27–28		
3:29		
3:30		
14:17	a ~~fool~~ is quick to anger. A man of wicked devices is hated	
15:1	grievous words stir up anger	soft answer turns away anger
16:28–29	sowing strife + whispering	
19:3	a ♥ that frets against the Lord	
22:24–25	friendship with an angry man	come away — don't fellowship with

21

Verse(s)		Source of Anger	Antidote
26:17	✓	Meddling in strife belonging not to him	don't meddle
26:18–20	✓	A MAD MAN casting firebrands, arrows+ death	?
27:4	✓	envy	
28:25	✓	pride stirring up strife	

A. Put a checkmark by any which are sources of anger for you. Pick one and describe why it's a sin for you.

I put a check by those that made sense to me before I got to this "?".
One that is a sin for me is Grievous words stir up anger in me. (esp. directed toward me or abusive)

B. Also describe the situations when the temptation seems strongest.

Out of the blue when I least expect it.

4. How are people described in Proverbs 4:14–17 who seem to enjoy making conflict?

They do not try avoid it. They deliberately enter into the path of the Wicked

A. Why do you think people enjoy making conflict?

Anger produces adrenaline that gives a rush feeling that is enjoyed for the moment - Sin nature loves it.

B. When are you tempted to create conflict?

when my ♡ is not surrendered.

Lord will you help me? answer this one? I know I am tempted to create conflict but when?

22

Some people actually do thrive from creating conflict. She may not realize she is using another person's reactions for her own purposes, but there could be a variety of reasons, most unclear even to herself. She may feel like she is in control when others seem out of control. She may crave the attention even if it is negative attention. There could be mental illness motivating her. If there is chaos around her, she may hope someone else gets blamed, not herself.

5. Proverbs 6:12–14 gives a visual description of the actions of a person who creates conflict and anger. What do you think each phrase means?

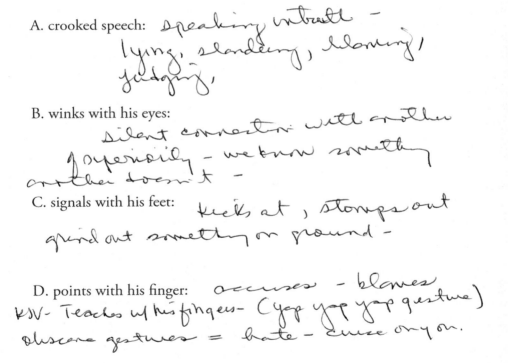

A. crooked speech: Speaking untruth – lying, slandering, blaming, judging,

B. winks with his eyes: silent connection with another of superiority – we know something another doesn't –

C. signals with his feet: kicks at, stomps out grind out something on ground –

D. points with his finger: accuses – blames
KJV – Teaches w/ his fingers – (yap yap yap gesture)
obscene gestures = hate – curse on you.

Although these "signals" may not be evident or used often in our current society, such physical expressions were particularly common in the cultures of the Old Testament. Through body language, one man signaled his accomplices how to deceive another person or take advantage. The victim might regard the behavior as benign unless he understood his oppressors' motives. Solomon is warning his readers to beware of flattery, teasing, lies, and laziness. Of course, such deception is possible today, even if it is uncommon.

6. How do the following verses from Proverbs say you should respond to the kind of people described in Proverbs 4:14–17 and 6:12–14?

A. 3:30: Don't strive with

B. 12:14–20: Speak the truth

C. 15:1, 18: Soft answer, slow answer –

D. 16:32: Slow speech + rule your spirit.

E. 17:14: Leave of contention

F. 25:21–22: Be kind - give food + drink to –

7. How could the truths of the following Proverb verses help create a surrendered heart that avoids conflict?

A. 1:8: Obey your parents

B. 1:23: Repent when corrected

C. 10:12: Love covers sin – (hate stirs)

D. 12:14–16: Speak truth hearken to counsel

E. 15:23: speak Words applicable to the situation – Speak a word at the right time. (a word in due reason)

F. 16:1–3: commit your works to the LORD & your thoughts shall be established.

G. 16:4, 16:33, 21:1: The LORD hath made all things for Himself The LORD has made the wicked for the day of evil. whatever lot, comes to me is of the LORD My ♡ is in His hands.

8. Do you think it's possible to avoid all conflict?

no

A. If not, do you think there's such a thing as godly conflict? If so, how would you describe it?

yes - speaking the truth in love even if there is no response in the person to whom it is spoken or worse more hatred.

B. What situations or decisions do you think could bring a conflict impossible to avoid?

Mass murder shooter -

Sometimes God will lead us to take a stand for him and a conflict or misunderstanding results. The relational conflict is nothing we invited or wanted. It's from someone disagreeing with us or feeling uncomfortable about our position. Jesus was in many of those situations, and he responded in godly, yet strong ways.

Assessing whether our position was right or wrong can't be based on the response of others. We can only obey God and leave the results to him. Sometimes a conflict actually helps another person to evaluate his beliefs and conclude he doesn't follow or believe in God.

Jesus didn't change his stance because people were upset with him, even trying to kill him. The disciples had a hard time learning that. At one point the disciples said to Jesus, "Do you know that the Pharisees were offended when they heard this saying?" (Matthew 15:12). They really expected Jesus to change his tune and avoid the conflict. They felt threatened. Yet Jesus didn't do anything differently. His confidence came from following his Father's directions. We can have peace like Jesus did even in the face of misunderstandings, even a threat to his life.

9. We know we shouldn't bottle up our emotions, especially anger, nor should we express all of them. Have you learned anything from this lesson to help you keep a godly balance between those two extremes?

A surrendered ♥ speaks softly + slowly the truth at the right time and knows this thing is from God —

Bottling up + Blowing up

10. How does the wisdom of the verses in this lesson affect your response to another person's anger, a difference of opinion, or outright conflict?

Wisdom - doing the right thing at the right time for the right reason in the right spirit.

Women of the Bible

11. According to Philippians 4:2, who had a conflict within the early church?

Euodia & Syntyche — Paul wanted them to be of the same mind in the Lord

A. Why did the Apostle Paul want them to settle their conflict?

So they would be of the same mind in the Lord.

B. Even though we don't know what was going on, can you think of a basic spiritual concept for them to help?

Submit to one another out of reverence for Christ. Look to the interests of others before yourself.

12. According to Acts 15:36–41, who also had conflict?

Paul + Barnabas — sharp contention

27

13. Why do you think anger or conflict between church members is harmful

It opens door for Satan to get in a cause division.

A. to the church?

B. to the ministry of the church? *all*

affect

C. to the fighting believers?

Every single human being, regardless of how seemingly mild-mannered, feels emotions like anger and is tempted to want conflict. Such reactions are a part of being human even when we know God and walk closely with him. There is no shame if we feel unpleasant emotions, but we do have a choice in handling them.

Even strong and involved Christians in the early church, who the Apostle Paul had mentored, were struggling with conflict. And surprisingly, even Paul and his long-time traveling companion and co-pastor/missionary, Barnabas, experienced relational challenges. We don't know whether Euodia and Syntyche resolved their conflicts, but Paul and Barnabas did in time (Colossians 4:10). God used the separation to spread the Gospel to more areas. Conflict didn't prevent God from fulfilling his plan and we needn't feel out of control when we face the same thing. God is still sovereign.

The challenge is to surrender over and over again to God's leading and perspective. The Proverbs supply much needed wisdom, along with the rest of Scripture. We are not left alone.

My precious Princess and Daughter:

I don't want my children to fight among themselves because of misunderstandings or pride. There are principles in my Word I want you to stand strong in but not through anger and demanding your rights. Most often, those emotions do not honor me. They are used for your honor and exaltation. However, those who surrender their anger to me and respond in humility to slights real or imagined find I can change the other person.

Beloved child, if you are struggling in some conflict, will you examine your heart sincerely and honestly? Have I actually asked you to fight this battle? Is the issue really that important? Seek me. I will coach you on how to speak the truth in love. And I will empower you to do the right thing—if you will listen to me.

If you are standing strong at my request, I will use this conflict to bring glory to my name. It will not be wasted. Never forget how much I love you. You are a princess in my royal family on my royal mission.

Lovingly,
Your heavenly Father, the King

Lesson 3

Proverbs about Correction

An important part of learning wisdom is being corrected. Most of the time the thought of having our faults, sins, or weaknesses pointed out by God doesn't seem like a great idea at all. In fact, it might even be very intimidating and feel dangerous. It can seem to threaten our worth and value. That may be true especially if we were not disciplined in a loving way by our own parents. They couldn't look at our heart's motives and know the perfect loving and effective way to direct us to godliness. Plus, their own faults, sins, and weaknesses hindered their responses.

But God is the perfect parent. He knows exactly the best way to point out our ungodly heart issues for our good and his glory. He knows our heart and understands our needs and motives. He only has good intentions for us.

Let's see from a study of verses in Proverbs how we can have more confidence and cooperation with God's good intentions through reproving us and pointing us to godliness.

1. Think of a time when God corrected you. How did you feel and what happened? convicted - wanting to take another route
- The wrath of man does not work the righteousness of God - The night of while coming home from Tiffany's.
- the contending of charlie over the vision of zachariah + the lampstand —

A. How do you know when God is disciplining you?

I feel ashamed within - disturbed - lack peace - know im on the wrong road - need to turn around -

B. What impure motives or wrong actions has he pointed out in you recently?

Selfishness, controlling - leaning to my own understanding - impatience

C. How has his correction changed you and empowered you to make more godly choices? If it hasn't, describe why you think it hasn't. *I have not been surrendered*

2. Note the connection between the truth of Proverbs 1:7 with each verse in 1:20–31. What is God saying about how the wise will regard rebuke? What are the benefits of rebuke to the wise? What are the consequences of ignoring rebuke? (Not every point will be found in every verse.)

	How the Wise Regard Rebuke	Benefit(s) of Rebuke	Consequences for Ignoring
1:20	*They cry out for it*		
1:21			
1:22			
1:23	*They turn at it.*	*I will pour out my spirit to you I will make my words known to you.*	
1:24			

	How the Wise Regard Rebuke	Benefit(s) of Rebuke ↓	Consequences for Ignoring
1:25	receive counsel welcome reproof	God will answer	
1:26		when we call on Him	I will laugh at your calamity + mock when your fear comes
1:27			Distress, destruction and anguish
1:28			I will not answer.
1:29	Love knowledge + choose the fear of the Lord.		
1:30			
1:31		dwell safely vs.33 Be quiet from fear of evil	They will eat of the fruit of their own way.

These verses are regarded by commentators as descriptions of Jesus, the holy Son of God. Only Jesus is perfectly wise, because he is fully God even while being a human on earth. He demonstrated God's wisdom by doing the right thing in every single situation on earth. He never made a mistake and he knew exactly how to respond to the actions of others—every single time.

Although we will never be able to respond perfectly on this earth because of our humanity, we can learn more and more how to grow in wisdom.

Many verses in the Bible talk about wisdom, and based on verses like Proverbs 1:7, 20–31, we see how important such growth is. It is God's call to us, knowing we will be more joyful while facing life and also more trusting of our heavenly Father who knows what is best for us. If you want wisdom, learn from Proverbs and also study Jesus's life whom the Apostle Paul was inspired to describe as "the power of God and the wisdom of God" (1 Corinthians 1:24).

Even as we are challenged to grow in wisdom, we can be comforted to know that as a part of our inheritance in Christ, we are already considered wise by God. Paul was inspired by the Holy Spirit to write, "And because of him you are in Christ Jesus, who became to us wisdom from God, righteousness and sanctification and redemption" (1 Corinthians 1:30). Paul also wrote, "'For who has understood the mind of the Lord so as to instruct him?' But we have the mind of Christ" (1 Corinthians 2:16).

Do we always respond like that's true? No, and God doesn't expect we will. But he is purifying us more and more by pointing out our ungodly reactions and teaching us how to walk in his power.

3. Why does God correct his children (3:11–12)?

Because He loves them —

    A. What does God want his children to do when corrected by him (4:1)?

Hear and seek to know understanding.

    B. Why should someone want to be corrected by God (4:2)?

Because God gives good doctrine — (not "that way" — "this way" — His way) always leads to what is helpful — better beneficial.

Being corrected or disciplined by God can <u>come in the form of any number of circumstances and/or people</u>. Maybe we are fired from a job without cause. Maybe a friend gossips about us. Maybe we are persecuted for our faith in Christ. Maybe we experience physical pain from a car accident.

Yet <u>not everything difficult is necessarily God's correction</u>. We don't need to assume circumstances always point to our wrongdoing. But <u>every</u> challenge is indeed <u>God's invitation</u> for <u>greater godliness</u> because <u>we must seek him in order to react in a loving and kind way.</u>

4. Read Proverbs 5:1–10. If the immoral woman represents any temptation, how does temptation work?

This passage paints a powerful picture of the sin of sexual lusts. The father exhorts his sons to stay pure and resist temptation because sin only ends in destruction. Since Solomon is the primary writer of Proverbs, we can safely say he is telling his many sons to beware. How ironic that Solomon was an immoral man with many wives and concubines. Even though he enjoyed God's gift of a prosperous and peaceful reign, he made many unwise choices. Most likely he experienced the destruction he's writing about and wants to spare his sons.

If we expand Solomon's intentions to point to any kind of temptation, we can see how the warnings apply to us. Every person struggles with temptation about something and to some degree. Even Jesus was tempted (Matthew 4:1–11) and was the only person who didn't succumb. We cannot expect to be sinless like Jesus, but these verses alert us of the intricate ways temptation lures us.

For instance, just as an immoral woman speaks (verse 3) as if her offer is good and sweet like honey, giving in only brings painful consequences and bitterness. Verses 5–6 could refer to the suggestion heart examination or discernment are not needed. Just "go with the flow." Verses 7–8 guide a person to stay far afield from sin by not even getting close to the attraction of evil.

Doubtless Solomon's wisdom resulted from his own wrong and right choices. Though he failed, God didn't give up on him. Even if we fail, God wants to forgive us and correct us to create spiritual strength and future faithfulness.

5. Read Proverbs 5:11–14. Have you ever regretted hating discipline? If so, what were the circumstances?

A. What happened?

B. How does knowing God will correct you out of love and concern motivate you to obey?

Solomon looks back and sees his errors. He rejected the wisdom of his father's advisors and chose "yes" men to advise him. And he didn't listen to the Spirit of God within him pointing out the follies of his choices.

Although we may not think we are "hating" God's discipline, we might be resisting it in subtle ways by becoming angry with someone who points out our ungodly response. Or we might try to explain away a biblical principle we don't want to obey. We can blame our anger, discontentment, bitterness, or any other ungodly response on others.

6. How is a lack of discipline (correction) linked with evil deeds (Proverbs 5:21–23)?

A. What truth does verse 21 give us for motivating us to obey God?

B. How do you want to apply it to your current situation?

7. Read Proverbs 6:23. How are God's words a lamp and a light in your life?

   A. Why are they important when understanding God's ways?

   B. Why are they important when learning from the consequences for sin?

Without the wisdom of the Bible, none of us would know the God–pleasing way resulting in the fruit of the Spirit: love, joy, peace, patience, kindness, goodness, faithfulness, gentleness, and self-control (Galatians 5:22–23). Just as every child must be taught the right ways to act, every one of us grows through biblical instruction.

8. What do the following Proverbs say about the positives of cooperating with discipline and the negatives of refusing correction?

	Positives	Negatives
10:8		
10:13		
10:17		
12:1		

	Positives	Negatives
13:10		
13:13		
13:18		
15:5		
15:31–32		
29:1		

A. Which of these positives is most important to you?

B. Which of the negatives have you experienced?

C. What did you learn from the experience?

D. What current change(s) are you making to avoid those negatives?

9. Read Proverbs 15:12. Why do you think people resist correction or warnings?

A. What has prevented you from listening to warnings in the past?

B. How does maturity affect your perspective of discipline or correction?

Every single person resists correction at one time or another and to some degree. We naturally resist wanting to feel or be seen as incorrect, inadequate, stupid, or any other of a multitude of unpleasant feelings. As children, we learn we don't like those feelings. No wonder since much of the time, authority figures give us the idea they think we can't change. Or some children are accused unjustly. Or the consequence is not commensurate with the level of wrongdoing. All parents, teachers, and others make these mistakes.

God never does. God's perfect purpose in correcting us is for our future good behavior, to assure us we are his children, and he cares about us. Hebrews 12:6 tells us, "For the Lord disciplines the one he loves, and chastises every son whom he receives." Then the writer of Hebrews continues, "For they (parents) disciplined us for a short time as it seemed best to them, but he (God) disciplines us for our good, that we may share his holiness. For the moment all discipline seems painful rather than pleasant, but later it yields the peaceful fruit of righteousness to those who have been trained by it" (Hebrews 12:10–11).

What is the "fruit of righteousness"? The Apostle Paul tells us in Galatians 5:22–23: "But the fruit of the Spirit is love, joy, peace, patience, kindness, goodness, faithfulness, gentleness, self-control; against such things there is no law." Those are for our welfare.

Anyone who keeps in mind God's good intentions will be able to avoid being the resistant scoffer Proverbs 15:12 talks about.

10. When a person reaps the consequences of a rebellious lifestyle, why does she often blame God (19:3)?

A. Have you ever done that? Why?

B. Did it help or hurt the situation?

Pride can often be the source of wanting to blame God. We like to think of ourselves better than we really are. We might think, "Well, if God would only change my husband, I wouldn't be angry." Or "I am entitled to criticize my boss because he doesn't acknowledge my efforts." Blaming God or someone else seems to take away our own responsibility. In those moments, we can choose humility, which acknowledges none of us are without fault. Only Jesus was perfect.

11. What wise approach to correction do you find in Proverbs 27:5–6?

A. Can you give at least one example of how you have seen the truth of these statements?

B. What kind of person do you resist correction from the most?

Often, we resist correction most from the person who seems to indicate they never do anything wrong and sometimes, don't even struggle. We can feel condemned and discouraged, as if there's no hope for us.

We can remember every person struggles and fails. Only Jesus is perfect. God never compares us to anyone. He wants us to seek only being more like Jesus and being empowered by the Holy Spirit to grow in righteousness.

Our loving heavenly Father knows we are weak. The Psalmist wrote, "For he knows our frame; he remembers that we are dust" (103:14). After all, he created us to need him. By keeping our eyes on Jesus and not the seemingly perfect behavior of others, our faith and trust in God will increase.

Women of the Bible

12. Read Acts 5:1–10. Do you think this was the first time Sapphira and Ananias had been dishonest? Explain your reasoning.

A. What principles from Proverbs can be seen illustrated in their lives?

B. Why do you think God disciplined Sapphira and Ananias so severely for their lies?

C. How do you think the fledgling church and the Christians in Jerusalem benefited from seeing this?

D. What impact does this incident with Sapphira and Ananias have on you?

Sapphira and Ananias's sin was not keeping the portion of land. They were not obligated to give all their land to the Christian community. Others gave their own land out of a generous heart. This couple's sin was their heart motive. They lied so that others would see them as generous and worthy to have influence within the community. Whether or not they were true believers, they hoped to gain something without trusting God to provide it in his way and timing. They were hypocrites and without correction, they would pollute the fledgling community.

Their death was necessary because the new Christians needed to see the extreme danger of such behavior coming from a hypocritical heart. And it's possible both of them had a stroke or heart attack because of the shock and fear of being exposed.

13. How will the truths in this lesson about correction affect you …

A. at work?

B. at home?

14. How has your perspective of correction changed as a result of this study?

Being corrected doesn't seem like fun, and we naturally want to resist what God intends for our good. If we keep the benefits of the fruit of the Spirit in mind, we will be more cooperative. Discipline is like a gift God offers for us to enjoy life and represent him in righteousness.

My precious Princess and Daughter:

I understand how hard it is for you to recognize the love behind my correction. At the time, you feel only the pain. But will you look beyond to see my love? I want you to grow and change for the better. I truly want you to be the best I know you can be in my Spirit's power.

Rebellion and resistance hurt you, my beautiful daughter, much, much more than any aspect of my discipline. Disobedience can destroy your joy, witness, and even your life. I don't want that to happen. Special One, I want you to enjoy your earthly life. I gave it to you with a wonderful purpose in mind. The more you follow my commands, the more fulfillment you'll find.

Try to see my correction in your life as positive, my child. There is no anger in my heart toward you—only love, even when I feel deep sadness because you insist on your own way. But even in the pain of correction, can you feel my hug of peace and love? I will never do anything not for your best.

Lovingly,

Your heavenly Father, the King

Lesson 4

Proverbs about Money

Money! We can say we love it or hate it, but it's always a part of earthly life. It has the potential to rule us or be used for God's blessings. Most often it is both, making it confusing and perplexing. How can we sort through our heart's desires about such an attractive temptation? We can't forsake it completely. It must be a part of living.

Thankfully, God knows the potential for temptation or for blessing. He refers to money a lot in the Bible. Approximately forty percent of Jesus's parables deal with money. There are more Scripture verses about money, more than two thousand, than any other topic. In contrast, there are about 500 verses on prayer and faith.

No wonder God inspired Solomon to extensively deal with the topic of money. Solomon often did use money wisely but ironically, also failed in major ways. Both God's directions and Solomon's experiences form the foundation for what we study here in Proverbs.

1. Some people put great value on their financial status or condition. On a scale of 1 to 5 (5 being most important), how would you rate the importance of money in your life?

A. In one sentence, write down your philosophy about money.

B. In one sentence, write down what you believe God's perspective of money is.

C. In what ways are those two perspectives similar and different?

2. What is one thing God regards as more important than money (Proverbs 3:13–15)?

A. What else is important to him (8:10–11)?

B. Why are these more important than money?

C. What do you think is the primary difference between God's view of money and most of humanity's view of money?

The wording of "earthly treasures" (Proverbs 3:13) gives the biggest clue as to the value of wisdom, instruction, and knowledge. Although technically we won't take wisdom, instruction, or knowledge into eternity with us, (although maybe we will), those elements will produce God's impact in the lives of people here on earth, and people will go into eternity.

The words "profit" and "gain" of most translations omit a significant meaning within the original: merchandise. Solomon contrasts the "merchandising" of wisdom and the "merchandising" of money. It's the idea of trading for gain. They both bring gain in different ways. Elements of earthly living like money, fame, and respect from others bring a kind of gain, but the results are fickle, undependable, and unsatisfying over the long haul. In comparison, wisdom, instruction, and knowledge bring greater contentment and the fruit of holiness in our spiritual walk, which is stable and satisfying, even when the lives of others are not affected as we would desire.

3. What does God say about wealth in these Proverbs verses?

A. 10:2–3:

B. 10:4:

C. 10:22:

D. 11:4:

E. 11:16:

F. 11:18:

G. 11:28:

Many of these proverbs may seem untrue since they aren't always completely fulfilled. The wording can seem unequivocally guaranteed because words or phrases like "most of the time," or "sometimes" are not included. They are blanket statements which feel "all or nothing." But we can keep in mind Solomon is stating generalized observations about God's ways, which is applicable about any Proverbs subject.

4. How can Proverbs 11:24–25 be applied in your life?

A. What results would you expect?

B. personally:

C. spiritually:

5. Could Proverbs 13:7 explain why those expectations aren't fulfilled sometimes?

Trying to apply the ideas or principles of Proverbs can be confusing and perplexing. We can observe a selfish woman who is wealthy, yet happy, and conclude God's Word isn't true. Or a man who is generous and loves God yet experiences many unfortunate things.

But we don't know everything about that man or woman. We can't see her motives nor what she chooses behind closed doors. Nor can we know what God is trying to do in her life in order to draw her closer to him—even if it means supplying riches. And for the generous person who is bombarded with trials, we don't know how God is glorifying himself. Only having an eternal perspective of God's global and eternal purposes and understanding the Bible as a whole empowers us to trust God.

6. According to Proverbs 12:11, what is one reason some people lack financial resources?

A. What other reasons can you think of?

B. In contrast, what is one biblical method to gain wealth (13:11)?

7. What is another key to being profitable and what hinders it (14:23)?

Of course, we know many jobs require talking—talking well and convincingly. But Proverbs 13:11 is referring to a person who only talks and doesn't take appropriate action necessary for success.

8. Rewrite Proverbs 15:16 by including things important to you. For instance: "Better to have a small cottage and love the Lord than a huge home and hate."

A. How can what you've written help to develop contentment within you about money?

B. What prevents that contentment?

9. How would you relate the truths of Philippians 4:11 and 19 to your current financial condition?

A. to your financial goals?

B. to what's most important to you in life?

C. to your attitude toward your salary (if you have a paying job)?

D. If you are a stay-at-home mom, your "salary" is less tangible. What is your "pay" and how does it relate to Philippians 4:11, 19?

10. Why do you think people covet money, sacrificing time with family or even honor to get it?

11. People do try to get money in dishonest ways. From the following verses, describe those ways (an activity) and something else about it (i.e., what God thinks of it or will do about it), if something else is included in the verse.

Proverb	Activity	God's Words
15:27		
16:8		
17:23		
21:6		

51

Proverb	Activity	God's Words
21:17		
22:16		

A. In what way(s) do these verses speak to you?

B. Do you need to make any changes because of those verses?

12. Having wealth isn't always a benefit. What disadvantages does Proverbs 19:4, 6 talk about?

A. Have you ever seen those disadvantages in your own life or in the life of another?

B. How did you or that person handle it?

13. How does God expect you to use whatever amounts of money he has entrusted to you?

A. 19:17:

B. 21:13:

C. 21:26:

D. 28:27:

14. What are important, godly attitudes about money?

A. 15:6, 27:

B. 22:1, 4:

C. 23:4–5:

D. 28:6:

E. 28:8:

F. 28:11:

15. What attitude(s) does God want us to have toward those with less money (Proverbs 22:9, 16, 22–23)?

Almost every person compares themselves to someone else and feels poor or wealthy. They might judge themselves poor and be tempted to self-pity and discontent. Others judge themselves wealthy and feel proud and self-sufficient, even crediting themselves for their many possessions or big bank account. Proverbs reveals God's perspective. He knows we will only be content by keeping our eyes on the spiritual wealth and daily provision he generously offers when we don't deserve anything good.

16. What biblical principle do you find in Proverbs 21:20?

The reference to oil is significant because oil was one measure of a person's wealth along with their possessions. It signified the ability to provide for one's own household and guests because olive oil was used for numerous household tasks. The lack of providing for family, friends, or strangers in need of an overnight stay was a shameful thing in the community. Plus, the verse is subtly pointing to the ability to provide for the future of his family and pass along wealth to the oldest son. A man who didn't provide for his children's inheritance was considered foolish for he must have carelessly squandered whatever he earned or had been given by inheritance.

17. Read Proverbs 30:7–9. If that is a prayer you would like to pray, write it here in your own words.

Women of the Bible

18. Read Acts 16:11–15, 40. Lydia was a wealthy businesswoman who sold expensive fabrics. What kind of person does Lydia seem to be?

A. What does her attitude toward money seem to be?

B. What are some ways she followed the principles about money expressed in this lesson?

19. What added insight(s) does the Apostle Paul say in Philippians 4:11–13, which would add to these truths from Proverbs?

    A. Write down what you now believe is God's perspective about money.

    B. Look back at your answer to the same question on the first page of this lesson and compare. Have your answers changed or stayed the same?

20. As a result of studying this lesson, is there anything God wants you to do about the money he has given you?

    Our habits of money management reveal our motives and what we value. If we disregard the wisdom revealed in the Bible, we will make unwise choices. If we don't trust God, we'll possibly try to provide for ourselves at the expense of obeying God, thus working too much at the cost of our families and even our health. Considering the importance God places upon this topic in the Bible, we can be assured he knows it's the barometer of our heart's spiritual condition.

    Our financial choices also indicate our beliefs about God and who he is. If we are stingy or fearful, we might believe God is impotent, unseeing, uncaring, incompetent, poor, or a myriad of other lies about his nature. But as we learned from Philippians 4:13, even the Apostle Paul had to learn to be content. Let us not become discouraged. God can redeem even our worst financial decisions. He wants to teach us, and we'll find the wisdom and direction we need in Proverbs.

My precious Princess and Daughter:

I own the cattle on all the hills of the earth and every ounce of gold inside the earth. Will you trust me to give you what I know you need? Remember, money is merely a medium of exchange, and in heaven's view, it has no value. It is just another way for you to grow as you learn greater trust in my caring generosity.

I know it's hard at times, my beloved child, to take an objective view of money and financial success. The world says your worth is tied up in money. But can you see that lie as one of the deceiver's traps? Money really has no value—except to serve my wishes and plans. Some day when you're in heaven, it will be of no use to you.

Valued daughter, I promise to provide for every one of your true earthly needs. Yes, I provide for each of my children in different ways, and you may wish I'd give you more, but will you trust me? It's so easy to compare, but I have a special and unique plan for each of my children.

More than anything else, you will inspire others with your growing confidence in my love about your finances. I will make it possible for you to live abundantly regardless of your earthly means. I'll be glorified through you. That is true riches—knowing I bless others through you.

Lovingly,
Your heavenly Father, the King

Lesson 5

Proverbs about Relationships

Some people consider interaction with people essential and energizing. Others value being alone and feel drained being with others. But we all must be around people. From the very beginning in the Garden of Eden, God said the man shouldn't be alone. Of course, he wasn't alone. The numerous creations of God had just been paraded before him, and he had named them. But he needed another like himself, and so God created his counterpart. Eve joined him.

Today, relationships can include relatives, friends, co-workers, casual acquaintances, or "friends" on social media. Any connection can be positive or negative, which God can use to bless or challenge us. But people were never meant to meet all of our needs. If they could or somehow did, we wouldn't need God. A relationship with God is the superior connection of life.

The book of Proverbs gives us succinct insights about relationships— more than you might expect. As we go through this lesson, keep in mind the Bible doesn't use the word "relationship," rather the word "friend." As you answer the questions, think of any relationship you want to apply it to. Be open to whatever God has in mind for you as the Holy Spirit enlightens your mind and heart.

1. How do you define a friend or a supportive relationship?

A. What are the characteristics you want most in that person?

B. What do you believe you best offer others in relationships?

C. Have you discovered anything new about yourself and your thinking by answering those questions?

2. What common quality (qualities) of a true friend does God show us in Proverbs 17:17 and 18:24?

A. What is another observation Solomon makes?

B. Do you find that idea confusing or helpful? Explain.

Both verses refer to the importance of a friend being faithful and true. Proverbs 18:24 wisely points out merely increasing the number of your friends doesn't necessarily mean you're increasing the blessings or the best support.

For one thing, having too many friends often occurs because we don't make wise choices of relationships. We include someone too quickly before we really know her well. We could be someone who craves lots of attention, and we may be too quick to tell someone too much about ourselves or entrust ourselves to an untrustworthy person. Our desperation diminishes our wisdom. Knowing what to share and how much comes from knowing our friend's heart and character over a period of time. Proverbs 17:17 and 18:24 set a wise foundation for building relationships.

Ultimately, we must remember only God is the completely faithful and true friend. Every human connection will fail us at some point, and at some point, we will fail others. Our friend may believe she has perfect motives in her interaction with us, but she may not truly understand the motives of her own heart. Or she may think she knows what is right for us, but we don't feel supported or loved. Only God knows perfectly what's for our best and has perfectly loving desires for us. He will never forsake us or be unfaithful or false.

3. How do the following Proverbs describe good friends and inadequate friends? (Not every verse will mention both).

Proverb(s)	Good Friend	Inadequate Friend
3:27–29		
12:26		
17:9		
18:1		
20:5		
20:19		

4. What does God say about the advantages of good friends and the disadvantages of inadequate friends? (Not every verse mentions both.)

Proverb(s)	Good Friend	Inadequate Friend
13:20		
27:9		
27:10		
28:23		

5. Why does gossip undermine a friendship (16:28, 25:9–10)?

A. In what other ways have you seen how gossip is destructive?

B. Why do you think gossip seems attractive?

Commentators tell us the verb "sows" in Proverbs 16:28 indicates the idea of sending forth like seed and "hurls as a missile weapon." The word "whisperer" is a graphic term we can picture in our minds. It has the idea of a person who hides her words and also her intentions. She can later defend herself by claiming she wasn't heard clearly.

Gossip seems like a tasty morsel because if we pass things along, we feel important. We know something someone else doesn't. Listening to gossip can make us feel needed or included in a special group, especially if we want to be favored by the gossiper, or we don't like the person who is the object of the gossip. Another motivator can be someone is entrusting us with important information. Then we feel even more important if we pass it along.

Another angle is our gossiping friend now values us because she may think we're supporting her. It's all a mess of sinful motives and we may not even be aware of what's going on in our heart.

In all of this, we are believing God created some people inferior and lower than us. We are defaming his image within that person. But every single person has been created in God's image, whether or not they acknowledge it. He created them with intrinsic worth and value even if they have smudged it themselves.

6. For many women this statement seems true: If you don't talk about people, what's there to talk about? How do you make sure talking about others doesn't become gossip?

A good way to determine whether we are gossiping is to ask ourselves, "Would I say this about her if she were standing here hearing it?" We can also ask God to reveal the motive of our heart. Do we hope to gain something or feel better about ourselves because we are a tale-bearer with seemingly the inside scoop?

7. What counsel does Proverbs 4:14, 18–19 offer as a basis for healthy relationships?

8. Read Proverbs 4:23–27. Although these verses do not necessarily refer to relationships, what basic and overall point do they make?

Everything we do, including any human connection or friend we choose and maintain, reveals the motives of our heart. If we are not choosing God as the ultimate provider for our emotional needs, we will demand from others what they cannot fulfill. When they fail us, we will be tempted to respond in ungodly ways. If someone, who we thought would make us feel special, rejects us, we may gossip about them. Or if we think our image in someone's eyes is less than we want, we may follow after them into sin to gain their approval.

These temptations are often subtle and alluring. We must be alert to quickly catch wrong desires within our hearts which will energize sinful responses.

9. What heart attitudes overcome the bitterness and misunderstandings that separate friends or destroy relationships?

A. 10:12:

B. 11:2:

C. 11:12:

D. 11:27:

E. 12:18:

F. 19:11:

G. 20:22:

H. Which of these heart attitudes is one you want to grow in?

I. How will you do that?

What an important and powerful word picture Proverbs 10:12 gives about anger toward others. We can "stir up" wounds or "cover" them with love and understanding, thus no longer being held in bondage by them.

If we choose to "stir up," we put the spoon of rehearsing hurts and misunderstandings into a pot of boiling mud and grime. Then we stir, stir, and stir causing any moisture of grace and mercy to evaporate. Then the mass solidifies into a hardened brick.

It's harder to resist throwing a hardened brick formed by bitterness and resentment after such rehearsing. We are easily tempted to hurl it at the offending party when she seems to be responding in hurtful ways. Or we think we feel better about ourselves by stacking brick after brick, building a wall of separation and distrust.

On the other hand, "covering" up is like taking the lid of that pot and securing it on top and throwing away the spoon. The lid is the forgiveness Jesus secured for us, which we did not earn nor deserve. We recognize how much we have been forgiven and must humbly apply it toward others.

No longer can we see the attractiveness of the boiling anger or have something to stir it with. Then we can gladly take the covered pot and throw it all away.

10. From each verse in Psalm 103:8–14, write down God's characteristics and/or actions which are an example for us to use in throwing away the covered pot.

A. vs. 8:

B. vs. 9:

C. vs. 10:

D. vs. 11:

E. vs. 12:

F. vs. 13:

G. vs. 14:

Of course, we can never act or respond like God in every instance, but we can grow in covering over our bitterness by choosing to give grace to others which was so abundantly given to us.

11. At times, a true friend refuses to help someone. Why or when would that be necessary?

A. 1:10–16:

B. 6:1–5:

C. 19:19:

D. 24:21–22:

E. Can you describe a time when you refused to help someone based on one of those principles? What happened?

It takes great wisdom and discernment to know when our friend is involved in something we shouldn't support. She may be convinced her decision is a good one, or it would be good for us to cheer her on. Obvious sin is easy to resist, but if it's something generally good, we also should consider the motive behind the desire. Does she want us involved because it's for her own pride, glory, image, or ambition? To refuse to help seems inconceivable to her because she is blinded to anything wrong in her own heart. But if we sense her muddy motives, we may have to refuse to help even though she doesn't agree or is angry. That's a very difficult choice, and it can often be done only because we have purified our own motives. Out of our own pure heart, if God wills, he can reveal our good motives in his timing to our friend.

12. Proverbs 21:14 may not seem like a good idea initially, but how could it be appropriate or necessary in some circumstances?

Although this verse can be difficult to decipher, giving a gift in secret shows the pure intent of the gift-giver. There is no one else to applaud or give praise. The receiver knows the gift is purely motivated for her good.

Thinking of the gift not just as a tangible item, but a gift of the heart makes this proverb even more powerful. Being forgiving, giving grace, and offering understanding are the kinds of gifts that put us in a vulnerable position. The person receiving the gift might refuse it. We could feel rejected or belittled. But if our eyes are focused on how God values us, we can risk our motives being misunderstood or our image being maligned.

13. Not everyone we meet has pure motives in relationships. What kind of people, circumstances, or connections do you think could apply to the situation described in Proverbs 23:6–8?

14. Sometimes we let jealousy or envy destroy a friendship or even turn into hate. Fill out the chart answering these two questions: What words describe a heart free from jealousy or envy? What are possible consequences of jealousy and envy?

Proverbs verse(s)	Description	Consequences
14:30		
24:17–18		
27:4		

15. How can you prevent jealousy and envy from taking root and growing in your heart?

16. Which of the qualities studied in the verses from this lesson do you value most in your closest relationships?

Women of the Bible

17. Read 2 Kings 5:1–14. How was the servant girl a friend?

    A. What potential obstacles or misunderstandings did she risk in order to show friendship?

    B. How could this girl's example be applied to friendships, especially in the workplace?

18. What discouraging and encouraging things have people said or done when you were having a hard time?

19. How can you help someone else right now?

The servant girl risked a lot, possibly her very life by speaking up and making a suggestion to her human master. We can only imagine how she must have depended upon and been strengthened by her Lord God, her real master, to take such a courageous action. She was a true and faithful friend who knew what was best for her master and represented God with wisdom and strength.

Proverbs has inspired us with wisdom and encouragement about how to love others and also honor God. Not all friendships will last forever, even the great ones. But some day in heaven, we will enjoy perfect fellowship as we interact with other believers. What a glorious day that will be. And the best part will be seeing our very best friend, Jesus our Savior, face to face and thanking him for making us his forever friend.

My precious Princess and Daughter:

Friendships are one of my many gifts to you. They lift you up when you're discouraged and increase your joy when you're happy. Yet, I never intended for friends to be a substitute for me. If you enjoy a person's company more than mine, something's wrong. I am the only one who can meet all your needs, the only one who can give you all the love you need.

I want you to have friends, to cherish the moments you spend together, to be there for each other, to seek their help. I particularly designed you as a woman to value relationships and to cultivate good ones.

When a friend blesses you, my loved one, know I am the source. When a friend disappoints you, know I am still there, offering my unconditional love and acceptance. Sadly, there are times when a friendship may be destroyed. But my love will never end. Nothing can separate you from my friendship.

Lovingly,
Your heavenly Father, the King

Lesson 6

Proverbs about Marriage and Parenting

We love our families, yet sometimes those very individuals offer the most challenges. That's often because we want so much from them—maybe too much. God did design family, especially parents, to represent him. But because of the selfish choices birthed in the Garden of Eden, sin made perfect representation impossible. Disappointment, anger, misunderstandings, and many other ungodly reactions are the results in the hearts of family members.

But none of that was or is a surprise to God who knew it all would happen. As a result, God supplied the perfect provision for our sins to be forgiven through the sacrificial death of his Son, Jesus. He also gave us biblical examples, although imperfect ones, which revealed we are not alone, and God wanted to help us. Proverbs gave the simplest and clearest instruction and insights for seeking and finding a healthy family, even if it's not perfect.

Someone has said an irregular person is anyone who thinks different or acts differently than us. Unfortunately, someone in our family is most likely thinking the same thing about us. Even more reason to see what we can learn as we continue to journey through the different topics Proverbs addresses.

1. What family relationships bring you ...

A. the most joy? Why?

B. the most heartache? Why?

2. When you got married or when anticipating having a child, what expectations did you have that ...

A. were met?

B. were not met?

3. Proverbs says a lot about wives. Why do you think that's so?

4. What do the following Proverbs say about women, positive and negative?

Proverb(s)	Positive	Negative
11:22		
12:4		
14:1		
19:13		
27:15–16		
30:21–23		

A. Of the good characteristics named, which do you see in yourself?

B. Which do you think your husband (or your friends if you are not married) values most in you?

C. Of the poor qualities or behaviors, which do you see in yourself?

D. Which ones do you think your husband (or friends) dislikes the most?

E. Which ungodly reaction have you been working on to correct and how have you been doing that?

5. It is true family members bring out the best and the worst in us. They also can be the most truthful about us. Share a time when a family member honestly shared with you an area where they believed you were weak or needed improvement.

A. How did you receive their comments?

B. Did you make any changes?

6. God created marriage. The union of a man and woman is very important to him. What does God say about it in …

A. 5:18:

B. 18:22:

C. 31:10–11:

D. In what one important way are you "good" *to* your husband?

E. In what one important way are you "good" *for* your husband?

F. In which of those areas mentioned in the verses in question 6 would you say you're strongest?

G. In which of those areas would you say you're weakest? How do you think you could improve?

7. What are the consequences for the marriage with an unfaithful spouse? (Although these verses refer to husbands, the same consequences are suffered by an unfaithful wife).

A. 11:29:

B. 22:14:

C. 23:26–28:

D. 27:8:

E. 30:20:

8. There are several verses in Proverbs using the technique of contrast to teach truths. For instance, "It is better to have _____ over/than _____." What do these verses say is better and, additionally, better than what?

Proverbs	The Better	Other/Than
15:16		
15:17		
21:9		
21:19		
25:24		

A. Which one of the contrasts is important to you for growth or change?

B. How would growth or change make a difference in your life/ marriage?

9. God addresses husbands. What are his instructions for them in these verses?

A. 2:16–19:

B. 5:18–22:

C. 6:23–29:

D. 6:32–35:

Ephesians 5:25 gives further instruction to a husband: "Husbands, love your wives, as Christ loved the church and gave himself up for her." Although Christ perfectly loved his church, the Body of Christ, a husband cannot do that. But he can grow in his selflessness and sacrificial love.

The challenge for you as a wife is to be content knowing your husband cannot perfectly fulfill that challenge. Any perfectionistic response to your husband's imperfections will only discourage him. If you are waiting for him to meet all your needs, you're more likely to complain and neglect being grateful for what he has done for you.

The apostle Paul tells wives in Ephesians 5:22, "Wives, submit to your own husbands, as to the Lord." Some versions use the word "respect" for submit. Your calling is just as hard as his, and you won't fulfill it completely either. Having grace and mercy and forgiving each other will go a long way in encouraging greater love and commitment.

The best foundation for being content and responding in godly ways is recognizing only God can meet all your needs, which he promises in Philippians 4:19, "And my God will supply every need of yours according to his riches in glory in Christ Jesus."

Also remember there is a difference between needs and wants. We all want a lot of things, which may or may not be what God calls needs. The wants are particularly dangerous in marriage because if we confuse needs with wants, we can begin to demand our wants must be met by our husband, or even God. Discontentment and complaining then seem reasonable, because we believe we're entitled. Only by trusting God has promised to meet our true needs can we be content in the midst of not receiving what we want.

10. God addresses the children of the family in Proverbs. What does God want your children to do or avoid?

    A. 1:8–9:

B. 13:1:

C. 15:5:

D. 15:20:

E. 19:26–27:

F. 23:15–17:

G. 23:19–22:

H. 28:24:

I. What can you do to help your children want to learn these things and obey God?

Sometimes our own past behavior as a child can negatively affect the way we respond to our own children or any child. If we were rebellious in childhood and suffered the consequences, we might overreact toward any child in our care. We might worry or react too strongly while giving consequences because we are determined to prevent that child from suffering consequences like we did. Or if we received strong consequences yet still rebelled, we might decide we need to be more soft-hearted.

Another influencing factor is how our spouse responds to our children. If a husband/father is very strict and lacks an emotional bond, we might be lenient to try to overcorrect. Or if the husband/father is largely unavailable, we might think we have to be both mother and father and over-correct with harshness.

Many moms and dads are terrified of responding incorrectly fearing they will ruin their child. They think they are totally responsible for all of their child's future choices. But all children are needy during and after childhood because of immaturity. Parenting is a challenging role, but we can grow in dependence upon God, who is the only perfect "parent."

11. As a child of God, how should you respond to his work in your life (3:11–12)?

A. What standard of obedience do you think he expects of you?

B. What attitudes mentioned in these verses can help you to want to obey God?

12. If you aren't faithfully obeying God, how do you think that might affect the way you respond to your husband and each child?

13. What does God say about disciplining children?

A. 13:24:

B. 19:18:

C. 22:6:

D. 22:15:

E. 23:13–14:

14. How does discipline, if it is done correctly (though imperfectly), strengthen family relationships?

    A. Why does it express love?

    B. How do you think a child feels who is not disciplined?

15. What does disciplining a child accomplish (29:15, 17)?

16. Just as God's discipline in our lives takes many forms, so should ours of our children. Do you think spanking can be done without anger and in a controlled, loving way? If not, why? If so, how?

17. What benefit does a spanking offer that other means of discipline do not offer, especially for a toddler?

There are many forms of disciplining children: logical consequences, natural consequences, time outs, withdrawing an activity or item, and spanking. Spanking is intended for toddlers because they don't understand other means. Plus, their attention span is limited, and they don't always understand an explanation in words. Spanking should never be done in anger. Even though they may not understand every word, you should still explain why they are being spanked (what was done wrong), affirm your love and use words like, "I'm spanking you so that you'll remember next time to obey."

If we are spanking in order to vent our own frustrations, we aren't spanking for their benefit, but for ourselves. Then we are more prone to act in hurtful ways, rather than ways of teaching and guiding.

18. If you were planning to teach a parenting class, what three things would you consider most important to communicate? (Answer only the categories you have experienced.)

A. parents of young children or first-time parents?

B. parents of teenagers?

C. parents of adult children?

19. What parenting skills would you like to improve?

A. How, where, and when will you seek help to improve?

B. When you think of improving, what negative thought seems to discourage you? What will you do about that?

We must be careful when making parenting improvement goals. They can become overwhelming if we set them too high to begin with. Our tendency might be to make all-or-nothing perfectionistic goals: "I'm never going to get angry again." "I'm always going to discipline correctly and biblically." "I'll always know the right amount of advice to give and what kind to give."

But these kinds of goals only discourage us because no one can improve one hundred percent, even if we've taken classes and read books. Instead of one hundred percent goals, think in terms of small steps, like, "I'm going to ask my friend to pray for me for patience during the late afternoon tomorrow because that's my hardest time to deal with my kids." "When my daughter willfully throws food on the floor, I'm going to calmly tell her lunch is over and take her away from the table even if I'm afraid she'll become hungry. Hunger will become the consequence and also the motivator to eat next time."

20. How does your faith in God impact the way you parent your children?

God never intended a parent to be perfect and meet all the needs of her child. Otherwise, that child would not need to look to God. Of course, we want to be as good a parent as possible. But an imperfect parent will need to believe God can redeem any mistakes she makes. Then he will receive the glory for his graciousness and power.

We all know adults who were raised in a dysfunctional family and yet walk with God in faith. We also know adults who were raised in emotionally and spiritually healthy families and aren't seeking God. An adult must face her own responsibility for the choices she makes. None of us can blame our parents because God is sufficient to restore whatever wasn't provided during childhood. Although we can't blame our parents, we can recognize how the emotional, spiritual, or physical wounds we received caused us to choose patterns of distrusting God. We must learn to heal and depend upon God.

Women of the Bible

21. Read Genesis 12:10–20. Do you think Sarai did the right thing in going along with Abram's plan?

22. How did God intervene and rescue Sarai from the consequences of her obedience to her husband? How does that speak to you?

23. Although God doesn't call us to cooperate with something dishonest, what basic principle is illustrated here about God's plan for marriage today (compare Ephesians 5:22, 33)?

24. What principles in this lesson do you think God wants you to work on in

A. your marriage?

B. your parenting?

C. your relationship with your parents and in-laws?

The example of Sarai can be confusing, even misleading, if you are being abused in any way by your husband. God never wants you to submit to being harmed or mistreated. You are a person of worth and value. That is proved by the complementing instructions for the husband and wife in Ephesians 5. Although we can't expect perfection, and we must allow for growth, the responses are intended to be for the other's good, just as God always intends our good. If you have any concerns or are wondering if you are being mistreated, please seek wise counsel. God wants to guide you to find the help and support you need.

My precious Princess and Daughter:

Relationships within a family can go from wonderful to difficult in a few months or hours—or minutes. I know. But your family is only one of my gifts to you. I do want relatives to be a mutual blessing and encouragement, but don't look to them as your primary source of love or joy. Only I can provide fully.

While your heart will long to love and nurture those in your family, don't place your husband or child on the throne of your heart. Please remember I am not just your heavenly Father—I am also your God. It is impossible for me to share my place of priority in your life. Don't let one of my gifts of family members take my rightful place as Lord and master. I know what's best for you. No one else does.

My valued child, if you are angry or bitter or resentful toward a family member, then forgive. Forgive as I have forgiven you. Release them from unrealistic expectations and the responsibility for your happiness or disappointments. You may discover if you do, they will seek your love and fellowship more than before.

Trying to control them will only make them turn away from you. But releasing them to my Spirit's power and work will open windows of blessings.

Lovingly,

Your heavenly Father, the King

Lesson 7

Proverbs about Trusting God

All of the Bible, including the Proverbs, leads us toward trusting God more. We see the truth about God: he is sovereign, all-powerful, totally loving, wise, kind, and sinless. By revealing who he is, in all his majesty, glory, goodness, and so many other magnificent characteristics, the Bible informs our mind and draws our hearts into worship, knowing he is worthy to be trusted.

As we act upon the truth about him and trust him more, we realize there are also benefits for us. It's not a one-way street. We realize we have more peace, joy, love, wisdom, and selflessness. The truth about God sets us free from fear and self-protection. We can relax and believe even if something seemingly bad happens, God has a bigger and wiser plan.

God wants peace for us. As we study biblical books like Proverbs, we begin making the connection between our ungodly reactions and how we aren't trusting God in that moment. We surrender, reminding ourselves of who our great and good God truly is. Our heart resets our spiritual compass to point to God. Let's examine Proverbs with that goal in mind.

1. As you look at the following areas of your life, rank your confidence (on a scale of 1 to 5, 5 being absolute) that God is in complete control. Base your answer upon your response when life doesn't go well in some way. Think in terms of your reactions over the last week.

work	ministry	a current crisis
children	friendships	dating or marriage
a needed decision	material provision	job

A. In two or three words, how would you describe your emotional reactions which could indicate whether you are trusting God or not?

B. In what way could you change your thinking about the certainty of God's control in each area?

It's very easy to say, "I trust God because I know he loves me." But sometimes our reactions indicate our trust and confidence isn't quite as deep as we thought. For instance, if you need a job and wake up at night feeling fearful, maybe there's some growth needed in your trust level. If you withdraw your heart from someone because you are afraid they will hurt you, maybe your trust is more in self-protection and less in God than you thought.

These things are very deep and require heart examination, which is not always easy. If we are responding in any way the opposite of the fruit of the Spirit, we aren't trusting God in that moment. Galatians 5:22–23 tells us, "But the fruit of the Spirit is love, joy, peace, patience, kindness, goodness, faithfulness, gentleness, self-control; against such things there is no law."

God doesn't say we should examine our heart in order for him to condemn us because in Christ, we are not condemned (Romans 8:1). The purpose of heart examination is to recognize how we're not including him in our thinking and motives. He knows ungodly reactions aren't good for us and others. He wants to make corrections, which will result in all the wonderful reactions of walking in the Spirit—for our good and his glory.

2. Why do you think Christians have trouble trusting God?

3. When you're having difficulty trusting God, what seems to be the primary cause most of the time?

4. When you're having difficulty trusting God, what seems to be the best remedy? Share both godly and ungodly reactions.

Often, we have a hard time trusting God because in our childhood bad or hard things occurred we didn't understand. Most often we blame ourselves as bad. Most children have a natural sense there is a God. Unfortunately, because of the hurtful things that occurred and our self-judgment, we think God can't love us. And since he allowed those bad things to happen, we think he intends our harm. That conclusion transfers into believing lies about God such as he isn't loving, kind, caring, or powerful.

For instance, a child may pray to God to help her, but when he doesn't do what she wants, she believes God doesn't love her, doesn't care about her, or is powerless to protect her. As a result, even after committing her life to God, the old beliefs can still affect her ability to believe God wants her best. She may not even realize she's believing lies. She just has an unsettled feeling.

Exposing the lies and replacing them with truth about God takes time and involves studying God's Word, being in community with other

Christians, and often counseling. It's a life-long journey of spiritual transformation, which never ends in perfection. Only in heaven will that sought-after perfection come.

5. In Proverbs, trusting God and fearing him seem to go hand-in-hand. Read Proverbs 3:5–8. How does God say to trust him (vss. 5–6)?

A. What is the opposite of trusting God (vs. 5)?

B. What are the results of trusting God (vs. 6, 8)?

C. What attitudes and behaviors help us trust God (vs. 7) and why do you think that's so?

D. What do you think it means to "fear God" (vs. 7), and why is that important for trusting God?

E. Which of the points in these verses are easiest and hardest for you?

The concept of fearing God is certainly one a child can misunderstand and which can be carried into adulthood. Every child experiences fears because the world is scary and confusing. Since a child can't process accurately the different meanings of "fear" in the Bible, it's easy for her to be as fearful of God as another person of authority who isn't totally loving or caring. The two can begin to be mixed up. As the child matures, she can diminish the lies about fearing God by having wise counsel and understanding the Bible's truths which are always accurate.

The Bible's concept of fearing God is not because he's like a scary person who is imperfect and prompts a cowering terror. This fear is an awe-inspired response based in his greatness and goodness, and his desire for the best for everyone. Such fear produces dependence, praise, seeking his guidance, and trusting his way is perfect. It comes from humility, acknowledging God is unbelievably bigger, better, wiser, kinder, more loving, and a vast array of perfect characteristics prompting us to bow before him. And we want to tell others about him because we want everyone to know this wonderful Lord and Savior who has delivered us from bondage to sin, even if we'll never conquer sin completely.

The opposite of that kind of fear is described in Proverbs 3:7 as being wise in our own eyes. We think we're better, smarter, and more loving than God. We trust ourselves and don't surrender to God's Lordship. We don't want to be needy and dependent upon him or those he might want to minister to us.

But when we are ruled by the right fear of God, we are motivated to "turn away from evil" (verse 7). Then our right choices will bring "healing to your flesh and refreshment to your bones" (verse 8). Even our physical condition can benefit from trusting God knows what is best.

6. How does memorizing God's Word empower us to trust him (22:17–19)?

A. Why does meditating on Scripture develop trust in God?

B. Describe a time when Scripture enabled you to trust God and respond in a godly manner.

7. Consider memorizing Proverbs 3:5–6. Place a check mark here if you intend to do that. _____ If so, indicate by what date. _____

8. If another verse would be more meaningful to you, indicate it here: _____. And the date by which you will have it memorized: _____.

9. One of the wonderful benefits of memorizing Scripture is greater trust in God. At the moment of not wanting to trust God, we can recall appropriately helpful Scripture. Indicate what each verse(s) says diminishes or encourages trust in God.

Proverbs	Diminishes Trust in God	Encourages Trust in God
14:2		
15:16		
15:33		

Proverbs	Diminishes Trust in God	Encourages Trust in God
23:17		
23:19–21		
24:3–4		
28:25		
28:26		
29:25		

A. Which of these have you experienced in your life?

B. Explain what happened?

10. From these verses indicate the consequences and/or benefits of trusting and fearing God.

A. 1:7:

B. 9:10–12:

C. 10:27:

D. 13:13:

E. 14:26–27:

F. 16:6:

G. 16:20:

H. 19:23:

I. What other benefits of trusting God have you experienced?

J. How do these verses encourage you to trust God more?

Knowing the benefits of trusting God can encourage us to believe God wants the best for us. At times, it's very difficult to trust because so much of life is confusing, uncertain, and conflicting. Things we want or feel are best aren't always what God chooses. Our inability to see the total, eternal picture blocks our understanding. But God graciously and patiently woos us to himself.

11. One way to increase our trust in and reverence for God is to concentrate on his wonderful attributes. How is God described in these Proverbs?

A. 3:19–20:

B. 15:3:

C. 16:4:

D. 17:3:

E. 21:30–31:

F. 23:10–11:

G. 24:11–12:

H. Why should the attributes of God increase trust in God?

I. What quality of God (either from that list or another verse) means the most to you right now as you trust him in a specific circumstance?

Studying, memorizing, and focusing on Scripture about who God is, may be for some, the core way to develop greater trust in God. We recognize his loving and wise hand upon us, even when bad or confusing things occur. We can refuse to believe the lies and instead rehearse the truth. We'll never know all of the reasons for the unfortunate things occurring on this broken earth, but in heaven, we'll see and understand God's loving work. Trust and faith in God's nature give us confidence to be content.

12. Scan 1 Samuel 1:1–2:11. What inspires you about Hannah's trust in God?

A. Notice God didn't condemn her for her feelings. How do you feel knowing your faith will not always be perfect and at times you will experience unpleasant feelings?

B. What lie about God's nature has contributed to you believing he doesn't want you to ever feel grief, loss, or sadness (if applicable)?

C. What truth about God's nature will you rehearse to help you?

D. What Proverbs verse(s) do you think Hannah would have appreciated the most?

13. What lessons of faith are most significant to you in 1 Samuel 1:1–18?

A. Why?

B. How will you apply those truths in specific ways or situations this week?

How wonderful to know Jesus, though perfect as a human and fully God, experienced and expressed feelings. The Gospel accounts (Matthew, Mark, Luke, and John) reveal his emotions didn't negate his deity. He understood the difficulties of life. He welcomes us to bring our emotions to him and deal with them in godly ways through trusting he will work for our ultimate good. Hebrews 4:15–16 assures us, "For we do not have a high priest who is unable to sympathize with our weaknesses, but one who in every respect has been tempted as we are, yet without sin. Let us then with confidence draw near to the throne of grace, that we may receive mercy and find grace to help in time of need."

Hannah's story tells us she went year after year to worship God and must have asked him many times for a child. Only in God's timing did she receive what she wanted. God doesn't always give us what we think is best, but he is still faithfully loving us and working for our good. Our challenge is to trust he knows better than us.

The Proverbs affirm how growing in trust in God is a life-long journey and process. The need to grow in our faith is God's invitation to depend upon him in deeper ways. If we suddenly had perfect trust, we wouldn't need to look to him at all. We could handle all of life without him.

The struggle of growth has a purpose. That doesn't make the journey easy. It is an adventure culminating in perfect understanding and trust in God when we reach heaven and know God without any obstacles.

My precious Princess and Daughter:

I am completely worthy of your trust. I am totally worthy to be feared. But I want your fear to be one of reverence and awe, not terror. I invite you to come boldly before my throne of grace. The more you get to know the truth about me, the more you'll be able to trust me and believe I know best and will bring about the best.

I understand your human, earthly viewpoint—our adversary, the devil, works hard to make you doubt I can be trusted. He did the same to Adam and Eve. Yet, I am more trustworthy than your certainty that when the sun goes down behind the horizon, it has not been swallowed by the sea and will rise again in the morning. Let that kind of strong confidence in the truth about me fill more and more crevices of your heart.

My love, care, and concern for you can never ever diminish. You are the object of my joy and affection, beloved daughter. Won't you rest in that love? I know you better than anyone and know what's best for you. You can believe I never punish you for being weak. I have realistic expectations of you. I created you knowing your weaknesses and struggles. I will be glorified as you learn to trust me more.

Keep your eyes on me, study who I really am, and rehearse those truths. I am the same yesterday, today, and tomorrow—and forever.

Lovingly,
Your heavenly Father, the King

Lesson 8

Proverbs about Pride and Humility

I hope I'm not the only one who allows pride to overwhelm God's gift of humility. Humility is truly his gift because he is the one who makes my heart willing to admit there's nothing within me deserving any praise. It's all of God, and he's the one who should get credit.

But then pride sneaks in because I choose to love someone unlovable, or I resist temptation, or someone thanks me for making a difference in her life. I try to thank God but now I feel like it's false humility. Oh! The complexities of being human are like a yarn ball of a thousand threads all jumbled together. The ends and beginnings of the strands are so hard to separate. The motives of my heart are just as jumbled.

How can we have the right perspective and response about pride and humility? How can we appreciate our strengths, acknowledge our weaknesses, and still cooperate with God's plan to use us and the wonderful spiritual gifts he's given us? Let's see how the biblical Book of Proverbs can help us.

1. How do you define pride?

A. How do you define humility?

B. Have you ever heard definitions of those concepts you disagreed with? Explain.

2. Why do you think it's hard for people to keep a humble perspective?

A. What seems to diminish a perspective of humility within yourself?

B. What helps to strengthen it?

3. What are the results of pride as described in these Proverbs verses?

A. 3:34:

B. 12:9:

C. 13:10:

D. 15:25:

E. 18:12:

F. 29:23:

The results of pride described in those verses sound like God's judgment, but they are his motivators for us to avoid pride because pride is not for our good. Pride fuels ungodly reactions which cause the destruction of relationships and failure in our ability to trust and obey God. To maintain our mask of pride, we must diminish our view of the worth, value, and capability of others. And our selfish heart usually spills out in destructive ways.

Regarding Proverbs 12:9 in the list above, some commentators believe the concept of the verse refers to the time and culture of Near Eastern and Asian cultures when even a poor man who worked hard could afford a slave. The verse is suggesting a humble working man can be rewarded with a slave, in contrast to a proud man who is unsuccessful and can't afford one.

Other commentators disagree and believe the wording refers to a humble man who supplies for his own needs by working hard. In contrast, the proud man refuses to acknowledge his failures and insists he is lacking nothing.

Proverbs 15:25 refers to the border of a widow's land. She is in humble financial means thus unable to fight against the proud man who tries to take over her land or move the boundary marker. In the Israelite culture, owning your family's land from generation to generation is essential. The helpless widow often only has God to defend her. And when he does it's sometimes to the point of literally or symbolically destroying the assets of the proud man.

4. What characterizes pride?

A. 21:4:

B. 21:24:

C. 24:17–18:

D. 25:14:

E. 25:27:

F. 27:2:

G. 28:13:

Proverbs 21:4 can be difficult to understand because the word for "lamp" (ESV, NASB, and others) can also be translated "plowing" (NKJV). Either way, it refers to the outward evidence of self-earned success in which the owner takes great pride. Only a rich man can afford a lamp, rather than a candle. A proud man also shows off a plowed field. Having a lamp or plowed field wasn't sin in itself, but Solomon is referring to a proud man whose motive is to show off his wealth. He doesn't give credit to God for his success but credits himself.

Proverbs 25:14 gives a comparison between a proud man who promises but never follows through. Just like clouds and wind seem to indicate rain but don't produce needed rain, both are disappointing and empty.

5. In contrast, what generates an attitude of humility?

A. 3:5–7:

B. 8:12:

C. 13:10:

D. 28:13:

E. 30:32:

How do you think humility strengthens someone in areas of life including relationships, spirituality, mental state, and physical health?

We tend to only focus on verses five and six when we look at Proverbs 3:5–7. But verse seven indicates the results of fulfilling the previous two verses: we will be able to be wise, fear God, and depart from evil.

As we study the Bible, we should be aware of the importance of studying Scripture in context. That means not focusing only on one verse or even a few verses, but studying a passage, chapter, or book of the Bible to see God's overall purpose and theme. Even knowing to whom the book was written can make a passage more understandable and diminishes the possibility of wrong interpretation and application.

The Book of Proverbs is unique because most of the time a verse is not connected in any way with the verses before or after it. It is a collection of ideas and thoughts which are observations of the way life operates most often. They are not promises nor guarantees. But when God is the source of the godly response a verse indicates, the good or bad things connected to it will more generally occur.

The phrase of Proverbs 28:13, "will not prosper," is not so much about materialistic provision, wealth, or poverty. Like other Proverb verses, this one contrasts good and bad. Therefore, confession and forsaking sin results in receiving mercy, but the person who doesn't confess and forsake "covers" his sin. The covering could apply to denying, hiding, or lying about it. Also, blaming others, making excuses, and any reaction which prevents someone from turning from their sin.

When a person isn't honest, she most likely won't receive mercy. Her heart won't prosper in the sense of gaining peace and joy and avoiding consequences. Real mind and heart prosperity come from admitting sin, receiving forgiveness and being cleansed, as I John 1:9 tells us: "If we confess our sins, he is faithful and just to forgive us our sins and to cleanse us from all unrighteousness."

Proverbs 30:32 includes the phrase, "put your hand on your mouth." That idea is only mentioned a few times in Scripture. The most famous time may be when Job repents and says it. It represents his awe of God and his repentance of having argued with and doubted God. There's also the sense of honoring God with silence, which requires self-restraint, especially for the person who is very good at defending herself.

6. What are the results of humility?

    A. 3:33–34:

    B. 11:2:

    C. 15:25:

D. 15:33:

E. 22:4:

F. 29:23:

G. Why do you think wisdom is an antidote to pride and reaps humility?

At the core, the proud believe they don't need God, and the humble are convinced they do. These proverbs refer not just to emotional pride versus humility, but also material pride verses lowly circumstances, like a widow. In all cases, a person who is proud believes they can do things on their own and that they know what is best. God knows such attitudes are not good for them. To be without God's help is stressful, creating ungodly reactions, tension, and even physical illness. God created men and women to need him. Humbly surrendering to dependence upon God brings peace, joy, and wisdom in responding to life and others.

7. Why do you think God hates pride (6:16–19, 8:13)?

In Proverbs 6:16–19, each of the God-hated descriptions are independent of each other, yet also related because they reveal the behavior and attitudes of a proud person. Of course, the list is not intended to be a complete representation of an evil or proud person, or to indicate all God hates. He hates any kind of evil because he knows it is not good for anything in his loved creation.

The numbered list of Proverbs 6:16–19 is a common literary device called *middah*, where items are listed but the final item is considered the worst of all. Proverbs 30:15–16, Proverbs 30:18–19, Job 5:19, Amos 1:3–2:1 and many other verses and passages use this form.

8. Why do you think God punishes the proud (16:5–6)? In what ways do you think such punishment might come?

9. What do you think pride indicates about a person's view of God?

10. Why do you think pride results in dishonor and shame (11:2)?

11. Why must humility come before honor (15:32–33)?

12. Do you think humility must be a process and not a one-time event? If so, why?

A person who doesn't trust God believes she must be in control of her own life. Pride indicates she thinks she is more capable than God. Trying to run her own life is a tremendous burden, but if she humbles herself believing God knows what's best, she can rest and have peace.

13. Why do you think Proverbs 16:18 is true?

A. Look up the definitions of "pride" and "haughty."

B. How are the two the same and different?

Some Bible versions have used the synonym of "arrogant" for "haughty." An arrogant or haughty spirit is one that disdains others and lifts up self. She loves strife to try to keep others off guard, loves being right, and believes her way is always and only the right way.

In the Bible, even when different words mean the same but are repeated, God is impressing the reader with the meaning's importance. The repetition indicates a stronger warning or encouragement.

14. What truth or life-principle do you think God is teaching in Proverbs 25:6–7?

15. What insight does Proverbs 27:2 give about being praised?

16. Read Proverbs 27:21. How do you think being praised tests a person?

    A. Which kind of responses to praise seem to bring even more attention to a person?

    B. What do you think is the best response to hearing praise about yourself?

    C. What do you think Proverbs 30:1–6 warns us against and as a contrast, encourages? Why?

Women of the Bible

18. Read Luke 1:26–56. How is Mary, the mother of Jesus, an example of a humble person? Give verses and characteristics.

19. How does she model a healthy humility without self-contempt? How does that speak to you for staying away from pride?

20. Mary could have been stoned for becoming pregnant while unmarried. How does her acceptance of God's will indicate a humble and surrendered attitude?

21. Do any of the verses or thoughts in this lesson help you diminish any area of pride or strengthen an area of humility? In what specific way?

Growing in humility and resisting pride is a life-long journey. We needn't feel discouraged if we fall back into old patterns. The challenge of thinking rightly about ourselves knowing God has given us his gifts and talents is a balancing act requiring wisdom. Continue to study the wisdom of Proverbs and your heart and mind will be fed with transforming truth.

My precious Princess and Daughter:

I love you! You are important to me. I loved you so much I sent my most precious gift, Jesus, to die in your place for your sins. Even if you had been the only person ever created, I would have done that for you. Just you. When you accept how much I love you and want the best for you, it will be easier for you to give humility a foothold in your heart.

Pride focuses on self. Humility focuses on me. Prides seeks self-promotion because a person believes I might not come through in an acceptable way. Humility seeks my glory, knowing I am the source of everything worthy to be praised.

Keep your eyes on me and be confident I'll let you know if you've slid over into pride. I know you'll never have pure motives. I have reasonable expectations. I will continue working within you for a humble heart bringing glory to me.

Serve others and remind yourself of how I'm empowering you. I will take care of honoring you, either on earth or in heaven. You will share my Son's glory in heaven regardless. But not because of your efforts but because you are empowered by him.

Regardless of any earthly accomplishments or failures, you are always my cherished daughter.

Lovingly,
Your heavenly Father, the King

Lesson 9

Proverbs about Love and Hate

God is love and God says to love. In fact, he says loving others represents him. We want to love so why is it so hard? And why do we find it easy to love certain people and not others? Certainly, loving others shouldn't be convoluted. Just love others.

But it's not easy, and it's hard to think of God loving everyone. Especially when the person is different and difficult, and sins against others or us. How can God say we should love *that* person?

As we'll find out in this lesson, God does mean *that* person. As we've seen in other lessons, Proverbs has a pattern of making contrasts. Now, we'll see how it applies to love and hate.

1. The word "love" is frequently used in our world and society, even misused. It has many meanings. How many meanings can you think of? Give examples.

2. How do you define authentic love?

3. We can love things as well as people. Who are the people and what are the things you love the most?

4. Someone has said the opposite of love isn't hate but apathy. What do you think? Why?

5. Can you think of any things or people you hated in the past and now love? What happened to change you?

Most of us grew up thinking of love as a feeling, sometimes only a feeling. We learned about love from television, movies, advertising, and now social media. God's view of love is a simple one: love is a choice for another's highest good. It may involve a feeling, but love doesn't have to be controlled by a feeling.

6. What does God say we should love (Proverbs 4:5–6)?

A. Why would he command us to do this?

B. In this command, how would you define love since it's not about a person?

In this command of loving wisdom, love could be defined as valuing, making time for, meditating on, obeying, and many other responses.

Jesus identified himself as "the way, the truth, and the life. No one comes to the Father except through me" (John 14:6). Wisdom is truth, and Jesus is fully truth. Many people replace the word wisdom in Proverbs with the name of Jesus as a spiritual exercise.

7. Read Proverbs 1:2–6. What are Solomon's purposes in writing Proverbs?

A. Which benefit do you need most right now?

B. Why?

The word for "wisdom" in Hebrew is in feminine plural, a personification of "the queen of wisdom." Wisdom supplies great benefits and advantages: knowledge of how to be godly, what is just, practical guidance (prudence), and spiritual maturity. Wisdom can be described as the right use of knowledge. It's not just knowing something but putting what you know into practice. This queen of wisdom cries out and weeps wanting good for humankind (Proverbs 1:20).

Jesus also, with great love, cried looking out over the city of Jerusalem because of its rejection of him as Messiah (Matthew 23:37). Jesus loved then and loves now his people and wants the best for them.

Paul identified Jesus as wisdom in I Corinthians 1:24, 30: "but to those who are called, both Jews and Greeks, Christ the power of God and the wisdom of God … And because of him you are in Christ Jesus, who became to us wisdom from God, righteousness and sanctification and redemption."

8. How does Proverbs 9:7–8 identify one of many reasons people might love or hate us?

We are to love others knowing it might mean calling them to righteousness. They may not love our exhortation and may respond negatively. Regardless, we must obey God and leave the results with him.

9. Read Proverbs 8:12–21. Identify the characteristics of wisdom which also describe Jesus:

A. vs. 12:

B. vs. 14:

C. vs. 15:

D. vs. 16:

E. vs. 18:

F. vs. 20:

G. vs. 21:

10. What does wisdom and Jesus hate and love?

A. vs. 13:

B. vs. 17:

C. What do you think motivates this love and hatred?

D. Hate is a strong word with negative connotations. Does it surprise you God can hate? Why?

E. Do you have an explanation for why God hates?

God's love is never for his own benefit as if we can provide something he needs. He is completely self-fulfilled and never uses us for wrong purposes. The glory we give him is because he deserves it, not to fulfill something he lacks.

11. What else does God hate?

A. 6:16–19:

B. 11:1:

C. 11:20:

D. 12:22:

E. 15:8–9:

F. 15:26:

G. 16:5:

H. 17:15:

I. 20:23:

J. Pick one of those hateful behaviors/reactions and explain how it could become a lifestyle pattern.

K. Which of those issues is a temptation for you? Describe how you will guard your heart and life from it.

L. Are you surprised at what God hates? How do your loves and hates compare to God's? What differences, if any, are there?

Proverbs 11:1 refers to a "just weight." The word "weight" is literally "stone" and the word "just" refers to justice. So the two words combined are a "perfect stone." Stones were used as a weight and the king had the correct weight of a stone. All measuring stones were to be measured against his. The sanctuary had its own set as Leviticus 27:25 indicates: "Every valuation shall be according to the shekel of the sanctuary: twenty *gerahs* shall make a shekel."

Second Samuel 14:26 gives an interesting background. "And when he (Absalom, King David's son), cut the hair of his head (for at the end of every year he used to cut it; when it was heavy on him, he cut it), he weighed the hair of his head, two hundred shekels by the king's weight."

By the time these Proverbs were written for Israel, commerce had become very robust, involving foreigners coming through the country for business. No longer did Israelites only use a "handshake" kind of interaction. There were more opportunities and temptations to be dishonest. Plus, the dishonest practices of foreigners influenced Israelites' businesses.

Although it may seem obvious why God would hate dishonesty, lying lips, wrong scales, hateful words, evil thoughts, and so many other things, he hates each one because he knows it will bring destruction onto his beloved creation. He isn't hating something just to hate it, but because sin doesn't reflect his justice, goodness, righteousness, and truthful ways. To be the just God he is, he must take action to stem ungodliness. Then others are warned against making unwise choices.

12. What else does Proverbs 17:5 reveal God hates?

Proverbs 17:5 could be misunderstood when it says someone shouldn't be glad at calamities otherwise, they will be punished. The idea is "he who is glad at the calamities of someone else will not go unpunished." There is the idea of mocking as the first phrase in the verse says. Such a person isn't loving, wanting the best for someone. God doesn't like this person because she mocks the poor and loves seeing the difficulties of others. No wonder God hates that and so should we.

13. What does God want us to love? Why?

A. 8:17:

B. 12:1; 15:9, 32:

C. 14:21:

In Proverbs 12:1, 15:9, 32, the word "instruction" includes correction, discipline, and understanding of the heart's motives. It's not information with no heart change and behavior change. God wants us to know why we make the choices we do, and to what degree we are being empowered by him or controlled by our own selfish wants and demands. If we don't examine and purify our motives, our selfishness will cloud our ability to know what is best for another person.

14. What does God want us to not hate (Proverbs 3:11–12)? Why?

15. Who hates God, why, and how do they show it?

    A. Proverbs 1:29–31:

    B. Proverbs 14:2, 31:

Proverbs 1:29–31 indicates people can hate God. Jesus tells us why in John 3:20, "For everyone who does evil hates the Light, and does not come to the Light for fear that his deeds will be exposed." And in John 7:7, "The world cannot hate you, but it hates Me because I testify of it, that its deeds are evil."

All of us tend to want to hide our sinful ways. We feel hopeless, unforgivable, ashamed, and unlovable. Satan wants to use those shameful feelings to encourage us to hide as Adam and Eve did (Genesis 3:8). But God wooed them and us by inviting us to come out of hiding and receive the provision of forgiveness of sin. For Adam and Eve, an animal's blood was shed pointing to the Messiah's death. When God sent Messiah Jesus to die on the cross for our sins, he knew every single one of them already. He isn't shocked or surprised. He has compassion for us (Psalm 103:13–14). Don't let those reactions prevent you from going to the foot of the cross and ask for forgiveness (I John 1:9).

16. Although Proverbs 5:15–23 is addressed to men, God wants any married person to have such a perspective about their spouse and resist temptations of adultery. What do you love most about your marriage?

A. If you are not married, what do you love most about the idea of being married?

B. How has making a choice to love your spouse or potential spouse been the most difficult?

Proverbs 5:15–23 graphically talks about resisting adultery and making marriage a priority. Satan is an expert at suggesting lies about love like, "The loving feelings are gone. There's no hope." "You really didn't love him to begin with, and he never loved you either." "You'll always feel unsupported, abandoned, and unloved."

Our enemy's primary lie is based in believing love is a feeling and not a choice. But God demonstrates true love. He didn't feel good about sending his beloved Son Jesus to the cross but out of a choice to love and demonstrate his love and grace, he did.

Don't go by your feelings whether you should stay married. And if you're not married but "in love," don't think those feelings will last forever or that they dictate who God wants you to marry. Feelings are fickle and fluctuating. Only the empowering of the Holy Spirit is sufficient for making a marriage last.

17. In practical ways, describe ways to love for another person's good in both aspects of Proverbs 10:12.

    A. hatred stirs up strife:

    B. love covers all offenses:

18. What loving choices do these Proverbs indicate?

    A. 16:13:

    B. 17:9:

    C. 17:17:

19. It may sound selfish to encourage loving yourself, but how does Proverbs 19:8 actually encourage you to do that?

The idea of loving ourselves, although biblical, can easily be misinterpreted and misapplied. Ideas range from "I'll put myself first" to "people must understand my needs and fill them." Any time we are insisting on being treated a certain way or upset if our needs aren't met, we aren't applying a correct biblical perspective. Only God can provide a true and accurate sense of loving ourselves by seeing our need of a Savior who describes us as precious, important, and valuable because of God's view of us; not our own self-analysis.

Women of the Bible

20. Read Mark 14:3–9. How did Mary of Bethany express her love for Jesus?

A. How do you express yours?

B. Have you ever experienced similar emotions in your devotion to God?

131

C. Have you ever made some kind of self-sacrificial act out of gratitude for all God has done for you? Describe the action and your feelings.

21. Now read Luke 7:36–50. Why was this act of love so meaningful to this woman?

22. What inspires your love for God or your love for others the most?

23. Based on the Proverbs you studied in this lesson, would you now define love any differently from your answer in the first question? Explain.

Love truly is a many splendored thing as the songs and movies tell us. God is love and because of his love, he created our beautiful world, creatures, and humans. Love is also complicated and complex. The wisdom Proverbs gives enlightens and empowers us to seek God to love more and receive love.

My precious Princess and Daughter:

Love is the sole motivation for everything I do for you. When I sent Jesus to the cross, it was because I love you. When I forgive you, it's because I love you. When I provide good works for you to do, it's because I love you. When I discipline you, it's because I love you. Out of my great love for you, I want you to share my love with others, and yes, even have a godly love for yourself.

Love is wanting the best for someone. It is desiring their good, not evil. It is choosing to reject bitter thoughts and resist hurtful responses. Only I can develop such a godly love within you. Be my channel of love to others. I will be glorified, and you will know your purpose.

Love others as I have loved you. Forgive others as I have forgiven you. This is the way of blessing. You'll never be sorry, and I will be pleased and honored before others as they see my work in your life.

Lovingly,
Your heavenly Father, the King

Lesson 10

Proverbs about a Woman After God's Own Heart

In our final lesson, let's look at a famous and powerful description in Proverbs 31:10–31 of the godly woman Proverbs highlights and lifts up as the ultimate woman of God. Yet, the positive description in those verses can be discouraging because she seems too good to be true. Can we ever attain such sacrificial selfless love along with unending energy and godly wisdom?

God doesn't intend to discourage us or give a perfectionistic image. His intention through his inspiring words is to challenge, yes, yet have an overall view of what life can be like. The passage covers the life stages of one woman not one day in her life.

God isn't expecting we will be perfect like this woman, but to depend upon him more and more. With the goal of becoming like this Proverbs 31 woman as much as possible, he wants us to grow in our godly qualities and righteous choices.

1. Read Proverbs 31:10–31. When you first read about this remarkable woman, how do you feel?

A. What do you immediately like about her?

B. What, if anything, do you dislike?

C. How are you similar to her?

D. What challenges you the most about her life as you compare it to your life?

2. How would you feel if Proverbs 31:10 could be interpreted as, "An excellent wife is hard to find. If you could find her, she would be like the following description"?

3. What qualities would you add to her description? Can you imagine why God decided not to include those?

Proverbs 31:1 tells us, "The words of King Lemuel. An oracle that his mother taught him." The word/name "Lemuel" means "from God" or "belonging to God," possibly referring to God providing baby Solomon to King David and Bathsheba as a reminder of God's redemption and restoration after their sin of adultery (2 Samuel 12:24–25, I Chronicles 22:9).

Therefore, some commentators believe King Lemuel is another name for Solomon, and this teaching is from his mom Bathsheba as advice for the kind of woman he should seek. As an adulteress herself, and maybe because she saw in Solomon some of the traits of her husband, David, she hoped he would choose the perfect woman for his queen. Ironically and sadly, Solomon ended up having many wives and concubines. Maybe he tried to find a wife who fulfilled every characteristic and couldn't, so he had to add more women to try to fulfill his every need. Or else the characteristics of so many women would add up to fulfilling Bathsheba's description.

The very fact the writer starts out saying, "who can find?" indicates it's impossible. Since no wife will ever be all this Proverbs 31 woman is (or at least for every moment of every day perfectly), we can be encouraged to know she can inspire us, but we don't need to compare ourselves as imperfect. God doesn't expect us to reach her example of perfection as verses in the New Testament indicate (Philippians 1:6, 1 Timothy 4:15, Hebrews 10:14). This woman should inspire us to grow but isn't intended to discourage us.

4. Proverbs 31:11–12 refer to marriage. Rewrite those verses with a practical description of what your husband values.

5. Does your husband trust you? If so, why? If not, why not?

6. If you're not married, what do you want your future husband to value most and how can it develop trust for you in him?

As modern women, we could easily take for granted a woman's valued place in our society, missing how this passage indicates God's value of women. The woman described is industrious, brings profit to the family, makes decisions, influences the community, and is powerful. Those were not the common characteristics or activities of women in Eastern countries. Women there were used and abused at their husband's whim and had no rights. But this Proverbs woman had power to make business decisions and control a household staff. In Eastern countries, a woman was a slave to her mother-in-law and had no rights. Her husband usually had no kind or positive thing to say about his wife in public.

For the weary mom of children today, the description of this "perfect" woman can be a source of discouragement. But we should remember we don't know when the Proverbs 31 woman did the different things described in these verses. It's highly unlikely she did them all at once.

7. From verses 13–24, what responsibilities does this woman have?

A. How do they remind you of your current life (in broad terms)?

B. What do you not relate to?

8. What management and decision-making responsibilities does she have (31:13–22, 24–27)? What does this say to you about God's view of women and their abilities?

God believes women are even more important and valued than society and the world currently regard them. The Bible is accused of being against women, their rights, and their value. But long before society regarded women as important, God indicated his value of women. Although his people, the Israelites, didn't esteem women the way he wanted, he provides for women who are oppressed. The Bible says a lot about taking care of widows, and the early Christian church obeyed (Acts 6:1–4). God is passionate about the care of his people, especially those who can't take care of themselves.

9. From the following verses in Proverbs 31, what personal character traits do you see in this woman?

A. 13:

B. 14:

C. 15:

D. 16:

E. 17:

F. 18:

G. 19:

H. 20:

I. 21:

J. 22:

K. 24:

L. 25:

M. 26:

N. 27:

O. 28:

P. 30:

Q. Whether married or single, which of these characteristics do you find most attractive and desirable for yourself?

R. Why would these qualities make you desirable as a wife?

10. When a man had a position at the gate (31:23), he had power and prestige in the community. How do you think this passage indicates she is involved?

The affairs of the community, including court, were carried out at the town gate. This verse points to how the Proverbs 31 woman is fulfilling her God-given tasks; therefore, her husband has confidence to know he won't be distracted unnecessarily by home problems or things she is not completing. It doesn't mean he isn't involved in his family, but when he is supposed to be at the gate and carrying out civic duties, he can concentrate on his assigned responsibilities.

Her husband's delegation of responsibilities to her reveal his opinion of her worth and strength. Those who don't know or believe God's value of women can easily forget this biblical woman has power, prestige, and makes decisions. She knows she has the power to affect the way people think of her husband and she wants only good for him, which is God's perfect design of a godly relationship. God is glorified by such a plan because it demonstrates his value of his created beings, both male and female, made in his image.

God's plan is timeless and when we look at this description of a godly woman, we see in broad categories, not much has changed. In the heart of people, we all are the same, wanting love, to be considered important and trusted to make decisions.

11. Create a modern-day scenario of one crisis, and then describe how this woman would respond to it based on Proverbs 31:25.

12. What would you like to apply to your own life from her example in Proverbs 31:26?

13. In our performance-based world, what do you think the "bread of idleness" (31:27) would be?

A. How do you know the difference between idleness and needed relaxation and recreation?

B. Can you give an example from your own life?

14. How have your children been a blessing to your life?

15. How would you like your children to bless you in the future (verse 28)?

A. Does your child's future expression of appreciation seem very promising? Why or why not?

B. What changes can you make to build a better relationship with your child?

Although the verb in verse 28 is present tense, this isn't intended as a promise for their whole lives. Even if a parent could be perfect, she would still have imperfect children who don't always appreciate their mom and dad. Every human sins and makes unwise choices. Every child must struggle to learn wisdom regardless how a parent responds.

The ultimate purpose is for each child to learn to seek God who is the only perfect being in their lives. God never intended for children to be robots without the ability to choose. For the most part, Proverbs 31:28 is referring to adult children who most likely have their own children. They've learned it was harder being a parent than they thought when growing up.

16. What would you like your husband's words to be as he praises you (verses 28–29)?

17. Of the three things mentioned in verse 30, which do you think you focus or depend upon the most (favor, beauty or fearing God)?

A. How do you feel when one of them seems threatened, unacknowledged, or unappreciated?

B. Does your focus and/or dependence need to change? If so, how?

18. Do your works praise you (verse 31)? If so, in what way?

A. How do you direct the praise to God, if indeed he really is the source?

B. If you want to acknowledge God but don't know how, what do you think might help or where do you want to seek help?

Women of the Bible

19. As you review the example of the Proverbs 31 woman, how does she inspire you in a fresh way?

A. How does she challenge you?

B. What does God want you to do about it?

20. As you finish this study of Proverbs, what does the prayer of Proverbs 30:5–9 mean to you? Which phrase is most important to you?

21. Consider praying the prayer of Proverbs 30:5–9, referring to yourself.

22. Why do you think God included Proverbs in his Word the Bible?

We have traveled through many topics found in the book of Proverbs, and yet, we haven't studied everything it includes. We can be more aware of the immensity of God's wisdom, greatness, and yet-undiscovered depths. No matter how long a person lives, even if she studied God and his wise ways her whole life, she could never fully know or understand God. God inspired Solomon and others to write Proverbs as a means of giving us a taste of God's true character and his perfect love, care, and pure motives.

Truly it's a challenge for us all to know God and learn his godly ways of responding to life and people. May we not take lightly the insights he has revealed to us in Proverbs.

As you've studied the Bible through this study book, you may have become aware you do not have a personal relationship with God and Jesus as your Savior and Lord. You've never seen your need for the forgiveness of your sins or you have been unwilling to admit your need.

If you would like to admit now your sinfulness and ask Jesus to forgive you based on his sacrificial death on the cross, you might want to pray something like this. "Heavenly Father, I am willing to tell you I need you. I have been determined to run my own life, or I've been trying to become perfect to earn your love. Thank you for loving me so much you sent Jesus to die for my sins and break the hold of sin in my life even though I haven't earned or deserve your grace and mercy. I acknowledge you don't expect me to be perfect on this earth, but you will welcome me as perfect in heaven. Please forgive me of my sins, cleanse me, and become my Master. Teach me your ways. I surrender to you. Thank you for making me your daughter, a princess in your kingdom. In Jesus' name, Amen."

If you made that decision, please contact me through my website: www.KathyCollardMiller.com. I would love to rejoice with you and also encourage you in your walk with Christ.

My precious Princess and Daughter:

I love to inspire you. I love to challenge you. I love it when you forsake your selfish will and are energized by my powerful Spirit, which can motivate you to holiness. I will enable you to be the best woman you can be. I know you'll never be perfect until you join me in heaven. But I intended the example of the Proverbs 31 woman to inspire you for your whole life.

There are different seasons of your life when I will assign you different tasks and responsibilities. Be open to those changes. Don't compare my plan for your life with anyone else's. I have given you many talents and many abilities. Learn deeper contentment as you use them throughout the seasons of your life to honor me. I am with you in every change, and my love is never based on your performance.

Daughter, are you listening? I love you with an all-encompassing, everlasting love. Never forget.

Lovingly,

Your heavenly Father, the King

About the Author

Kathy Collard Miller is best known for her practical biblical teaching with vulnerable sharing, humor, and motivation woven throughout her speaking and writing. Her ministry began when God delivered her from the sin of abuse of her toddler daughter and restored her broken marriage to Larry.

Her first book telling her story was published in 1984 and now has been revised and expanded as *No More Anger: Hope for an Out-of-Control Mom*.

Since her first book was published, Kathy has been in awe of God's plan to develop a ministry with a world-wide impact. She is the best-selling and award-winning author of more than fifty books, which feature a full array of nonfiction genres including Bible studies, Bible commentaries, and Christian living topics, and has also been an editor of compilation books. Some of her other books are *Pure-Hearted: The Blessings of Living Out God's Glory* and *Never Ever Be the Same: A New You Starts Today* (co-written with her husband, Larry).

Kathy's articles have appeared in numerous magazines and online sources. She has appeared on hundreds of radio and television programs including the *700 Club*.

Kathy is also amazed about the open doors God has given her for speaking. She has spoken in over thirty US states and eight foreign countries, including China, Indonesia, and Greece. She loves to see new sights and is so grateful her ministry allows her to travel and see the world.

Kathy and Larry married in 1970, are both lay counselors, and often write and speak together, especially at marriage events. They live in Southern

California and are the parents of two and grandparents of two. Contact her at www.KathyCollardMiller.com.

Books by Kathy Collard Miller with Elk Lake Publishing, Inc.

Christian Living Books:
Pure-Hearted: The Blessings of Living Out God's Glory
No More Anger: Hope for an Out-of-Control Mom

Daughters of the King Bible study series:
Choices of the Heart: ten lessons about the women of the Bible, contrasting two different women of the Bible about one topic in each lesson.
Whispers of My Heart: ten lessons about prayer.
At the Heart of Friendship: ten lessons about different aspects of relationships.
Heart Wisdom: ten lessons about different topics covered in the biblical book of Proverbs.
More books in the series will be forthcoming.

* Purposes of the tongue :

To Speak — To enunciate
To sing   To communicate
to swallow   to speak languages
to clear teeth
to whistle
To make obsene gesture (sticking it out)
to make noises
To roll "r's"
To speak { comfort
            warning
            encouragements
            direction
            guidance

misuses: Yelling
         ranting
         complaining
         grumbling
         gossip
         condemning
         scaring
         making fun of
         criticizing
         Speaking harshly —
         tearing down
         Speaking coarsely, lewdly —
         cursing

Made in the USA
Columbia, SC
30 July 2019